Seeking Wisdom

"Jann Aldredge-Clanton once again inspires us in our everyday work. The blessings and prayers she offers assist those of us in public ministry to provide the breadth and depth of Wisdom in the wider world. I heartily recommend these beautiful offerings."

—Karrie Oertli
ACPE Supervisor, Director Department of Pastoral Care
Integris Baptist Medical Center, Oklahoma City, OK

"For the preacher or worship leader seeking a fresh voice, unique twists in the language of liturgy, and many ways to articulate God's expansive essence, this book is a gift of spirit and intellect. Dr. Aldredge-Clanton artfully combines her years of ministry experience with her command and love of language to provide a timely resource for chaplain and pastor alike to breathe in Wisdom's counsel and then offer others words of grace and guidance."

—Nancy Ellett Allison
Pastor, Holy Covenant United Church of Christ, Charlotte, NC

Seeking Wisdom

Inclusive Blessings and Prayers for Public Occasions

JANN ALDREDGE-CLANTON

WIPF & STOCK · Eugene, Oregon

SEEKING WISDOM
Inclusive Blessings and Prayers for Public Occasions

Wipf & Stock
An Imprint of Wipf and Stock Publishers
199 W. 8th Ave., Suite 3
Eugene, OR 97401
www.wipfandstock.com

ISBN: 13: 978-1-60899-601-8

Manufactured in the U.S.A.

Scripture quotations, unless otherwise identified, are taken from the New Revised
Standard Version Bible, copyright 1989, Division of Christian Education of the National
Council of the Churches of Christ in the United States of America. Used by permission.
All rights reserved.

Scripture quotations identified RSV are taken from the Revised Standard Version of the
Bible, copyright 1952 [2nd edition, 1971] by the Division of Christian Education of the
National Council of the Churches of Christ in the United States of America. Used by
permission. All rights reserved.

Scripture quotations identified KJV are taken from the King James Version.

Scripture quotations identified MLB are taken from the Modern Language Bible,
The Berkeley Version in Modern English, copyright 1959 (revised edition, 1969) by
Zondervan Publishing House. Used by permission. All rights reserved.

In loving memory of Rev. Martha Gilmore,
who inspired me to become a minister and
who followed Wisdom's paths of peace and justice.

Contents

Acknowledgments xi
Introduction xiii

SECTION 1   INCLUSIVE BLESSINGS AND PRAYERS
                        FOR COMMUNITY SETTINGS 1

Interfaith Day of Prayer 3
Interfaith Community Thanksgiving Service 6
Martin Luther King Jr. Day Celebration 7
Habitat for Humanity Workers 8
Women's History Month Celebration 9
Holocaust Remembrance Day 10
Peacemakers Conference 11
University Commencement 12
University Board Meeting 13
American Association of University Professors Meeting 14
Interfaith Conference Banquet 15
Ministerial Alliance Meeting 16
Women Pathfinders Banquet 17
United Negro College Fund Banquet 18
Forum on the Elimination of Violence against Women
        and Children 19
Outreach Center Employees 20
Leadership Development Workshop 21
Rotary Club Youth Citizenship Awards Banquet 22
Business Dinner Party 23

SECTION 2 INCLUSIVE BLESSINGS AND PRAYERS FOR HEALTHCARE SETTINGS 25

Medical Center Chapel Dedication 27

Blessing of Hands (for people in the healing professions) 29

Blessing for Interfaith Healing Service 31

Blessings of Stem Cells and Marrow 32

Ovarian Cancer Survivorship Celebration 36

Teal Tea (teal: color for ovarian cancer awareness) 37

Breast Cancer Survivorship Celebration 38

Women Cancer Survivors Celebration Luncheon 39

Prostate Cancer Survivorship Celebration 40

Men Cancer Survivors Celebration Luncheon 41

Opening Meditation, Writing for Wellness Group (for patients, their families, and/or medical staff in a journaling group) 42

Transplant Survivors Reunion 44

Reproductive Health Center Reunion 45

Medical Treatment and Research Center Dedication 46

Breast Imaging Center Dedication 47

Medical Center Neo-Natal Unit Dedication 48

Interfaith Prayer Garden or Chapel Donor Luncheon 49

Remembrance Service (for people in the healing professions to grieve their losses) 50

Nursing Excellence Celebration 56

Medical School Graduates Celebration Dinner 57

Medical Staff Meeting 58

Medical Center Board of Directors Meeting 59

Medical Secretaries Forum Luncheon 60

Medical Center Auxiliary Board Meeting 61

Medical Center Volunteer Celebration 62

SECTION 3 INCLUSIVE BLESSINGS AND PRAYERS FOR FAITH COMMUNITY SETTINGS 63

Marriage/Union Ceremony 65
Marriage/Union Renewal
    (for one or many couples together) 68
Rehearsal Dinner for Marriage/Union 69
Baby Dedication 70
Memorial Service 74
Lay Ministers Dedication 77
Praise Dance Performance 78
Denominational Annual Conference or Convention 79
Ordination to Ministry 80
Advent of Wisdom 83
Beginning an Inclusive Faith Community 85
Mother's Day Celebration 87
Calls to Worship 88
Invocations 96
Prayers of the People/Pastoral Prayers 103
Offertory Prayers 138
Benedictions/Closing Blessings 143

SECTION 4 INCLUSIVE BLESSINGS AND PRAYERS FOR VARIED SETTINGS 149

Earth Day Intergenerational Celebration 151
Groundbreaking of a New Worship Place 153
Thanksgiving Celebration 154
House Blessing 156
Beginning a New Ministry 159
Prayer for People Suffering
    from a Human-Made Disaster 160

Prayer for People Suffering from a Natural Disaster 161
Healing Meditation 162
Transition of a Colleague to a New Ministry 164
Wisdom's Blessings 167
Lamenting Injustices 168
Lamenting Violence against Women and Girls 170
Call to Justice and Peacemaking 173
Call to Freedom 175
Diversity Celebration 177
Wise Aging Celebration 179
Blessing Our Creativity 182

Acknowledgments

M Y DEEPEST GRATITUDE GOES to the gracious people and communities with whom I have been privileged to serve as minister. The patients, staff, and colleagues with whom I have served at Hillcrest Baptist Medical Center in Waco, Texas, and Baylor University Medical Center in Dallas, Texas, have blessed me with their wisdom and encouragement. My appreciation also goes to the Waco Conference of Christians and Jews, the Waco Ministerial Alliance, and to the entire interfaith communities of Waco and Dallas. To the members of St. John's United Methodist Church (now Central United Methodist) in Waco, Pullen Memorial Baptist Church in Raleigh, North Carolina, and other faith communities around the country where I have had opportunities to lead worship, I am indeed grateful. My appreciation also goes to the academic communities of Baylor University, Texas Christian University, Southern Methodist University, Perkins School of Theology, Richland College, McLennan Community College, and Paul Quinn College.

My thanks also to Susan Carlson Wood for her expertise in editing my manuscript, and to Christian Amondson, Tina Owens, James Stock, and Raydeen Cuffee at Wipf and Stock Publishers for their fine work on this book. They have been responsive, encouraging, and talented publishing partners.

Introduction

O N THE MORNING OF September 11, 2001, I had just begun my chaplain rounds on one of the oncology units at Baylor University Medical Center in Dallas, Texas, when I got the news that hijacked passenger jets had crashed into the twin towers of the World Trade Center and the Pentagon. The first patient I visited pointed to her TV, and we watched together in shock and horror. My beeper went off, and I ran out to the nurses' station to return the call. The director of our Pastoral Care Department was asking me to help plan a hospital-wide interfaith prayer service to take place at 11:00 a.m. It was now about 9:30 a.m. I was frantic to hear from my son Chad, who at that time was flying from a political consulting job in Buenos Aires, Argentina, to an interview in Columbia, South Carolina. The news reports were filled with fears that terrorists may have hijacked other planes. How could I concentrate on planning a service? But I gathered with other chaplains, who asked me to give the opening prayer at the service. I got back to my office about 10:45 a.m. I still hadn't heard from Chad. I had only fifteen minutes to write this prayer and get to the auditorium on the seventeenth floor of another building in the Medical Center to open the interfaith service.

There have been times when you also have been called at the last minute to give a prayer or blessing. These may have been times of great stress or other momentous times in the life of an institution or community. It would have been helpful to me on that September 11 morning and on other occasions to have a book of interfaith prayers to consult. This collection of inclusive interfaith blessings and prayers comes to you with the hope that it may help you in a variety of settings.

Whether you are clergy or layperson, you are called upon to give prayers and blessings for various public occasions. In more than twenty-five years of ministry in the roles of hospital chaplain, interfaith conference director, parish pastor, and pastoral counselor, I have been asked to bless a wide range of events, such as ovarian cancer survivorship celebrations, the installation of a hospital hyperbaric chamber, interfaith conference banquets, Martin Luther King Jr. Day celebrations, Women's History Month celebrations, Holocaust Remembrance Day services, university commencements, baby dedications, remembrance services, and medical staff meetings. You will find these blessings, the September 11 "Prayer for People Suffering from a Human-Made Disaster," and many others in this book. Here you will find more than two hundred inclusive blessings and prayers for public occasions.

The blessings and prayers in this book use gender-inclusive language for humanity and divinity. They also include and respect people from diverse religious traditions gathered in a variety of public settings. Predominant themes are peace, justice, healing, liberation, partnership in relationships, and caring for the earth. You will find prayers for overcoming injustice based on race, gender, class, religion, sexual orientation, and disability. These blessings and prayers include a wide variety of divine images to suggest the vastness and all-inclusiveness of Deity.

As the title of this book suggests, a prominent divine image in these blessings and prayers is that of Wisdom. This is an ancient image, common to many religious traditions. Wisdom is *Hokmah* in Hebrew, *Hikma* in Arabic, *Sophia* in Greek. But Divine Wisdom has for the most part been stifled, demeaned, or ignored for centuries. Our world is in deep need of the healing that Divine Wisdom can bring. Upon receiving the Global

Environmental Citizen Award from Harvard Medical School, journalist Bill Moyers said, "The news is not good these days. What we need is what the ancient Israelites called *Hokmah*, the capacity to see, to feel and then to act as if the future depended on us. Believe me, it does."[1]

Twenty years ago I preached a sermon with this introduction: "What ever happened to Wisdom? In all my years growing up in Sunday school and church I never heard of God as Wisdom. I never heard God referred to as 'She,' even though the Bible uses Wisdom as a feminine personification of God. In much of human history Wisdom has been sadly missing. Instead of Wisdom, we have had injustice. Instead of Wisdom, we have had wars. Instead of Wisdom, we have had hierarchy and greed. Instead of inclusive images of Diety that affirm all human beings as created in the divine image, we have had exclusive images that devalue half of humanity—females. We need a faith that includes worship of feminine Wisdom so that there will be justice for females and for all human beings. Without Wisdom we all suffer. Wisdom brings power for change. She leads us on paths of peace. She is better than gold or any wealth or approval. In a world of divisions and brokenness, wars and violence, Wisdom can bring peace and wholeness."

In the years since I preached this sermon, much of my ministry and writing have been focused on seeking Wisdom. Divine Wisdom continues to bring new revelations in my personal experience, and I am more convinced than ever that our world is in deep need of her peace and healing. My hope is that the blessings and prayers in this book contribute to seeking and finding Wisdom. The book of Proverbs confirms the rewards of finding Wisdom: "Happy are those who find Wisdom, and those who get understanding, for her income is better than silver, and her revenue better than gold. She is more precious than jewels, and nothing you desire can compare with her. . . . Her ways are ways of pleasantness, and all her paths are peace" (3:13–15, 17).

Wisdom leads us on paths of peace. The prayers and blessings in this collection seek Wisdom so that we can be peacemakers. Wisdom will show us ways to use our unique gifts to contribute to peace in our communities and in our world wounded by violence.

Wisdom leads us on paths of justice. The inclusive blessings and prayers in this book seek Wisdom for overcoming injustice. Wisdom can help us create a world of justice and shared power. Wisdom and other feminine divine images give sacred value to women and girls who for centuries have been excluded and ignored, even cursed and abused. In the United States alone, every fifteen seconds a woman is battered.[2] One in three women in the world has been beaten, coerced into sex, or otherwise abused in her lifetime.[3] Worldwide, an estimated four million women and girls each year are bought and sold into prostitution, slavery, or marriage.[4] Seventy percent of the world's poor are women.[5] Balancing feminine and masculine names for divinity gives strong support to the equal value of women and men of all races. The divine images in our prayers and blessings can lay a foundation for overcoming gender, racial, and other forms of injustice.[6]

Wisdom leads us on paths of partnership: partnership among faith communities, partnership among women and men, partnership among races, partnership among people of all sexual orientations, partnership among people of various abilities. The prayers and blessings in this collection seek Wisdom's guidance for partnership in relationships. Imaging partnership between the feminine and masculine Divine can provide a foundation for human partnerships. In sacred texts we discover metaphors of masculine and feminine divine partnership. Hebrew Scripture pictures Wisdom (*Hokmah*) in creation, "beside [*Yahweh*], like a master worker" (Proverbs 8:30). The Qur'an in numerous places describes Allah as "exalted in Power, full of Wisdom [*Hikma*]" (14:4). In Christian Scripture we find reference to Christ as the "power of God and the Wisdom [*Sophia*] of God" (1 Corinthians 1:24). Inclusive divine images inspire commitment to peace and social justice through shared power.

> Sister Spirit moves around us; Brother Spirit joins in love;
> She and He together dancing, crowned with holy Heavenly Dove.
> May we join this dance of freedom, making heaven and earth anew.
> All our gifts will blossom fully as our dreams come into view.
> Sister Spirit gives us power; Brother Spirit ends all strife.
> She and He together lead us to a spring of flowing life.
> May we drink this gift of healing from a Giver wise and true.
> Now our voices join in shouting, "Come and see all things made new."[7]

Seeking Wisdom: Inclusive Blessings and Prayers for Public Occasions is designed for clergy and laypersons in community settings, healthcare institutions, and faith communities. The first section includes blessings and prayers appropriate for various town or citywide events, such as a Community Thanksgiving Service and a Martin Luther King Jr. Day Celebration. In section one you will also find blessings for universities, businesses, Habitat for Humanity groups, ministerial alliances, Women's History Month celebrations, Holocaust Remembrance Day services, and other community settings. Section two focuses on healthcare settings. Among the blessings you will find here are those for breast cancer survivorship celebrations, prostate cancer survivorship celebrations, medical center volunteer banquets, transplant survivors reunions, chapel dedications, nursing excellence celebrations, and interfaith healing services. The third section focuses on faith communities. Among the blessings and prayers in this section are those for memorial services, baby dedications, marriage/union ceremonies, ordinations, and lay minister dedications. Section three also includes prayers of the people or pastoral prayers, calls to worship, invocations, offertory prayers, and benedictions. In section four you will find blessings and prayers that may overlap in their use in community groups, healthcare institutions, and faith communities. Included in this section are blessings for beginning a new ministry, justice and peacemaking, wise aging, diversity training, groundbreaking for new worship places, and Earth Day celebrations. Section four also includes a lament for violence against women and girls and a lament for other forms of injustice.

In this book you may find other prayers and blessings that you think appropriate for multiple settings. For example, you may want to use the blessings for Martin Luther King Jr. Day and Women's History Month in community-wide, healthcare, and congregational settings. You may see other overlapping applications of blessings and prayers. You may want to adapt or combine some of these blessings and prayers to fit specific occasions. This book is intended to spark your creativity and to expand your repertoire of blessings.

Seeking Wisdom: Inclusive Blessings and Prayers for Public Occasions comes with the invitation to explore the creative possibilities in the opportunities you have to bless others. It is my hope that all our blessings and prayers will guide people to Wisdom's paths of peace, justice, and partnership.

ENDNOTES

1. Bill Moyers, "There is No Tomorrow," from remarks upon receiving the Global Environmental Citizen Award from the Center for Health and the Global Environment at Harvard Medical School, *Star Tribune*, January 30, 2005, 5.

2. "Broken Bodies, Shattered Minds: The Global Epidemic of Violence against Women," *International Journal of Epidemiology* 30 (2001) 649–52. Online: http://ije.oxfordjournals.org/cgi/reprint/30/3/649.pdf.

3. United Nations General Assembly, "In-Depth Study on All Forms of Violence against Women: Report of the Secretary General, 2006," A/61/122/Add.1 (July 6, 2006). Online: http://www.unifem.org/gender_issues/violence_against_women/.

4. The United Nations Population Fund, The State of World Population 2000 report, "Lives Together, Worlds Apart: Men and Women in a Time of Change" (2000). Online: http://www.unfpa.org/swp/2000/english/ch03.html.

5. Louise Arbour, United Nations High Commissioner for Human Rights, "International Women's Day: Laws and 'Low Intensity' Discrimination against Women" (March 8, 2008). Online: http://www.ohchr.org/EN/NewsEvents /Pages/DisplayNews.aspx?NewsID=8629&LangID=E.

6. Jann Aldredge-Clanton, *In Whose Image? God and Gender*, revised and expanded ed. (New York: Crossroad, 2001), 1–4. In this book I give biblical, theological, and historical support for inclusive images of God. I demonstrate how reclaiming biblical divine feminine images and including them along with masculine and non-gender images in worship contributes to healing women, men, children, and the earth.

7. Jann Aldredge-Clanton, *Inclusive Hymns for Liberating Christians* (Austin: Eakin Press, 2006), 20–21.

Inclusive Blessings and Prayers
for Community Settings

INTERFAITH DAY OF PRAYER

(held in an interfaith chapel or an interfaith prayer garden)

OPENING PRAYER FOR PEACE

Leader: Divine Wisdom, we come seeking your guidance in our efforts to work together for peace. We come from diverse ethnic groups, cultures, and religions. We believe these differences enrich us all. Lead us on your paths to lasting and true peace. Holy Wisdom, show us your pathways to peace in our own hearts, in our communities, and in our world. Grant us your peace to resolve our personal internal and external conflicts. And may your divine peace that surpasses all human understanding flow from us to our community and to our country and on to our world. May we be good stewards of the resources you have given us as individuals and as a nation. Guide us to use these resources well in relationship with our world. Help us to give equal respect to all people—women, men, and children of all races, cultures, and religions in all nations. For we are all created by you in your own image, and we are all precious to you. May we join hands as sisters and brothers in this community and around the world to work for peace, to heal divisions, to break down walls, to end oppressive systems. Give us grace to join your holy work of making peace on earth as we continue to become all you created us to be.

RESPONSIVE PRAYER OF COMMITMENT

Leader: Gracious Maker of us all, we commit ourselves to giving mutual respect to everyone in order to help bring peace and understanding among people of different religions, ethnic groups, and cultures.

All: We commit ourselves to celebrating our religious, cultural, and racial diversity and to making more opportunities for greater understanding.

Leader: We commit ourselves to creating dialogue, so that there will be an increase of mutual trust and cooperation among individuals, among communities, and among nations.

All: We commit ourselves to working for justice and freedom for all people, so that there can be true peace in our world.

Leader: We commit ourselves to forgiving one another for past and present prejudices and injustices.

All: We commit ourselves to supporting one another in our common efforts to overcome all forms of discrimination, hatred, greed, and violence.

Leader: We commit ourselves to taking the side of the poor and the oppressed, to speaking out for those who have no voice, and to working effectively to change these conditions.

All: We commit ourselves to promoting friendship and solidarity among people, for we are convinced that increased understanding of one another will bring peace and justice.

Leader: We commit ourselves to urging leaders of nations to work together for peace based on justice. For "how very good and pleasant it is" when we recognize that all people of the world are sisters and brothers, and we "live together in unity" (Psalm 133:1).

All: This prayer of commitment we bring to you, Loving Maker.

RESPONSIVE CLOSING BLESSING

Leader: May Divine Wisdom give guidance to all people.

All: May Divine Wisdom bless all people with peace.

Leader: May we go forth from this place remembering that all people—women, men, and children of all races, religions, and cultures in all nations—are created equally in the divine image.

All: May we join hands as sisters and brothers in this community and around the world to heal divisions and to build bridges of respect and understanding.

Leader: Go forth with wisdom and grace to join our Creator's work of making peace on earth as we continue to become all we are created to be.

All: So let it be, now and always.

INTERFAITH COMMUNITY
THANKSGIVING SERVICE

It is good to give thanks to you, Holy One, to sing praises to your name, to declare your steadfast love and faithfulness. May we experience your presence in fresh ways as we come together to build bridges of understanding and cooperation. In this worship service may we find new connections with you and with one another that we translate into deeds of justice and compassion.

Giver of Bountiful Blessings, we come with deep gratitude for health and strength, for opportunities to give and to receive, for eyes to see the beauty of a sunset and the sparkle in the eyes of children, for ears to hear music and laughter, for tongues to speak and to taste Thanksgiving feasts. But we also come to remember those children whose eyes cry out their need and whose ears too often hear the growling in their own stomachs and the fighting of those around them who are struggling in their poverty. Help us to feel the suffering of our sisters and brothers in need and to respond. Challenge us to join with you and with one another in breaking down barriers of prejudice, injustice, ignorance, and poverty so that all your people—female and male of all races and religions and nationalities—may have the freedom to become all you created us to be. Empower us with your love so that we can be your agents of change in our community and in our world, through your gracious Spirit. So let it be!

MARTIN LUTHER KING JR. DAY
CELEBRATION

Leader: "Injustice anywhere is a threat to justice everywhere,"[1] Martin Luther King Jr. wrote and preached. Dr. King used love and nonviolent resistance to work against racism, classism, and militarism.

All: Dr. King's words and actions inspire us today to work against all forms of injustice, including sexism, heterosexism, and ableism along with racism, classism, and militarism.

Leader: Yes! Martin Luther King Jr. wrote that all of us "are caught in an inescapable network of mutuality, tied in a single garment of destiny. Whatever affects one directly, affects all indirectly. I can never be what I ought to be until you are what you ought to be, and you can never be what you ought to be until I am what I ought to be. This is the interrelated structure of reality."[2]

All: Let us honor Martin Luther King Jr. today through non-violent actions against injustice anywhere. Let us work toward Dr. King's vision of a world free of discrimination and injustice in any form. May our words and actions help to create a world where all can be free to become what we are created to be.

Leader: Holy Wisdom, guide our celebration today. May the life of your prophet Martin Luther King Jr. inspire us to join hands as brothers and sisters of many races and religions to work toward the vision of justice and peace everywhere in our world. Let it be so!

HABITAT FOR HUMANITY WORKERS

Spirit of Love, thank you for bringing brothers and sisters of many races and religions together to build homes for families who need them. May the Habitat for Humanity workers here today feel the deep-down reward of knowing they are not only building a house, but they are building human dignity. They are helping to eliminate the depressing and debilitating cycle of poverty, and affirming the worth of all your creation. May these workers feel the reward of joining with committed people of faith throughout the country to build a more just and peaceful society by spreading this world's resources more equitably. May they feel the reward of joining you to build a more loving world. Help all the workers here today to feel your smile upon them. Bless and strengthen them as they build love, justice, human dignity, and unity. Amen.

WOMEN'S HISTORY MONTH
CELEBRATION

Leader: In the beginning female and male were created in the Divine image.

All: We affirm our faith in the divine image in all of our sisters and brothers.

Leader: Then women began to be looked down on as inferior, and they were dominated and enslaved.

All: We name this pattern of domination and slavery as sin.

Leader: Remarkable achievements are absent from our history books because they were done by women.

All: We name this exclusion as sin. We affirm our responsibility to write women back into history. We celebrate all our sisters who have gone before us to light the path of liberation and justice. We celebrate all our brothers who have stood by and for women.

Leader: We celebrate our sisters, like Sojourner Truth, and our brothers, like Frederick Douglas, who worked hard and long to free both women and people of color. They lived out their strong belief that all races of women and men are created equal.

All: We affirm our commitment to join hands with one another to reclaim our past, transform our present, and create a new tomorrow.

Leader: Let us ask the blessings of the Spirit of Life and Freedom on this commitment.

All: Sister-Brother Spirit, who inspires us all, come to our gathering here this day, as we celebrate women, past and present, too often ignored, maligned, cursed, abused, but who have overcome and remained faithful to the vision you have blazed within them. Light the fire of your vision within us, so that we too will be faithful to our calling, now and always.

HOLOCAUST REMEMBRANCE DAY

Gracious Mother-Father Creator, we have come together to remember your people who have suffered and died because of prejudice and hatred. As we remember the horrors of the Holocaust, renew within us the passionate determination to struggle with all our strength to ensure that never again will such suffering be inflicted on any people. But as we remember the sins of the past, we also confess our sins in the present—attitudes of distrust and scapegoating of those who are different from us, institutional racism and sexism, blaming the victims of injustice for the evils in our society, all attitudes and actions that diminish the worth and dignity of human beings and thus provide a breeding ground for violence and exploitation.

May we remember that we are all created in your own image and thus have the high honor and responsibility of sharing in your creative work of peace and love in our world. As we work for peace, help us to remember that there can be no true peace without justice. Holy Wisdom, guide us as we struggle for justice. Help us to join you in breaking down walls of oppression and in restoring our broken world to wholeness. Give us grace and power to right the wrongs of the past and present so that no one is denied opportunity because of religion, race, gender, sexual orientation, age, or disability.

We come not only to mourn the past but to affirm our hope for the future. We refuse to believe that hatred and strife and evil have the last word. Divine Wisdom, because we believe in your power at work within us, we believe that love and peace and goodness will prevail. Empower us as we dare to believe that by joining hands with one another and with you, we shall overcome. Amen.

PEACEMAKERS CONFERENCE

Hear the voice of the Divine Feminine, who has long been excluded: "I am Ruah, Breath of life. I am Hokmah-Sophia, Wisdom. I am a Fountain of blessings flowing freely through all creation. Come to me! Come to me! There is life in my words and healing in my touch." Let us listen to Her voice and feel Her touch. For the sake of truth and justice and peace and healing, let us worship the Feminine Divine. "Long we've needed Her embrace, glory and power of Her grace."[3] Now we gather up Her blessings as we celebrate Her many names: Ruah, Creative Spirit, Sophia, Hokmah, Wisdom, Sister, Shekinah, Mother Eagle, Friend, Black Madonna, Divine Midwife, Mother Hen, Birth-Giver, Comforting Mother, Housekeeper, Mother Earth, Divine Healer, Holy Mother, and so many more. "Look, look, for She is here; Her wisdom words have long been near. Now, now, behold Her grace, divinity in Her image."[4]

Great Creator of the universe, She and He, all in all, pour out your blessings upon us as we move forward with faith and hope to be your peacemakers. We dare to believe that you live within and among us, giving us power to change our world. We dare to believe we can be co-creators with you of a world of peace and justice, a world where all children, women, and men are free to become all you created us to be in your divine image.

> Come, Spirit who makes all things new.
> Show us your wider, fuller view.
> Teach us our wholeness now to see.
> Stir us to be all we can be.[5]

UNIVERSITY COMMENCEMENT

Our strong Mother and tender Father and so much more than we can ever imagine, we ask your blessings upon this celebration of achievement of mind and spirit. We invoke your presence as we honor these graduates who have used your gifts of intellect and talent to strive toward their potential. Thank you for families, professors, administrators, and all those who contributed to making their dreams reality. May feelings of accomplishment spark new dreams and goals. Challenge these graduates and all of us to use education and opportunity to open doors so that all your children may have freedom and opportunity to develop their minds and to achieve their goals. Inspire us through this celebration to continue to develop our gifts and talents and to use them to make a difference in our world. Amen.

UNIVERSITY BOARD MEETING

We praise you, Spirit who gives birth to all things new—new revelations, new opportunities, new life. Our hearts are filled with gratitude as we come together to take part in your continual creation. May the creative energy that comes from our connection with you and with one another inspire our work here this day and in the future. May we support and strengthen [name of university] as it continues to fulfill its mission of [mission statement of university]. Challenge us all to continue to develop our talents and to use them in service to humanity. Amen.

AMERICAN ASSOCIATION OF UNIVERSITY PROFESSORS MEETING

Gracious Giver, we gather today with gratitude for your abundant gifts to us. We are indeed grateful for all the educational opportunities you have given us—opportunities to learn and to teach. Thank you for the gift of freedom. Divine Wisdom, guide us to use your gifts as we continue to advance academic freedom and to ensure higher education's contribution to the good of our community, our country, and our world. Bless this meeting as we work together to become better learners and educators. May we all continue to become all you created us to be in your divine image. So be it.

INTERFAITH CONFERENCE BANQUET

Source of Truth and Justice, we celebrate your work within this organization and within our individual lives. We ask for a special awareness of your presence with us as we come together to build bridges of understanding and cooperation. Help us to feel the suffering of our sisters and brothers around the world who are denied basic human rights because of prejudice, ignorance, and greed. But keep us from becoming so overwhelmed by the magnitude of human suffering that we think we cannot make a difference. Rather, help us to commit ourselves more fully to uniting hearts and efforts to bring justice and healing and equal rights to all human beings. May we be filled with your love that embraces all creation. Empower us with this love so that we can be your agents of change in our community and in our world. Nurture us with this food and with our relationships with one another. In your holy name, we pray. Amen.

MINISTERIAL ALLIANCE MEETING

O Holy One of many names, we rejoice that you bring us together with a common purpose of working for justice and peace in our community. Bless us as we unite our talents and energy to make changes for the good of our community. As leaders in our faith communities and in our larger community, we seek your guidance for all our words and actions. May this Alliance be supportive, renewing, informative, and challenging for each of us. Thank you for the wisdom and encouragement we receive from one another. May we continue to grow together and to lead others to grow toward all we're created to be in your divine image. Amen.

WOMEN PATHFINDERS BANQUET

Giver of Life, our strong Mother and tender Father and so much more than we can ever imagine, we rejoice that we are all created in your own image. This evening we come especially to celebrate your image within women who have had the courage to walk down untrodden paths and to open closed doors, who have had the vision to create new opportunities for women and for men. We invoke your presence as we honor women who have been open to your Creative Spirit within them. Holy Wisdom, Sister Guide, lead us all on your paths of peace and healing. Challenge us to join with you in continuing to break down barriers of prejudice and injustice so that all your children—female and male of all races and religions—may have the freedom to become all you created us to be.

UNITED NEGRO COLLEGE FUND BANQUET

Author of all knowledge and truth, Source of all beauty and reason, we gather on this occasion to celebrate the minds you have given us and the educational institutions dedicated to developing and stretching our minds. We invoke your presence as we challenge one another to support and strengthen these institutions in their vision of providing greater opportunities for all people to reach our full potential. Empower and inspire us to join with you in continuing to break down barriers of prejudice and injustice and ignorance so that all people—black and brown and white, female and male of all faiths—may have the freedom to become all you created us to be in your divine image. Fill us with your love so that we can be your agents of change in our community and in our world. We thank you for good food and for all the ways you nourish our bodies, minds, and spirits. Amen.

FORUM ON THE ELIMINATION OF VIOLENCE AGAINST WOMEN AND CHILDREN

Loving Friend, who understands and shares our deepest suffering, we thank you for all those who have come here today because we want to be your ministers of compassion and your agents of change. Divine Wisdom, show us your vision of a world without violence and abuse. May we join you in empowering women and children to become all you created us to be in your image. Show us ways to help those who commit acts of violence against women and children, and to bring healing change for all. Teach us ways to change our religious and educational institutions so that all people are given equal opportunities and value, thus providing the foundation for eliminating violence against women and children. May we join you and one another in making your vision of peaceful homes and communities reality, so that we all can become the glorious, joy-filled creation you intended. May your life-giving grace and love be with us, now and always. So be it.

OUTREACH CENTER EMPLOYEES

Compassionate Spirit, we come today with gratitude that you live within and among those who work here at [name of the outreach center]. Give them fresh hope when they grow weary and discouraged. Often they may feel that no matter how much they do or how well they do, everywhere they turn there are still poor and hungry people. They may run out of food and money to pay utility bills, and even run out of emotional and spiritual energy for this ministry to needy people. Renew their strength. Keep alive the vision that led them into this ministry. Divine Wisdom, guide them as they care for hurting people and as they care for themselves. Empower us all with your vision of justice and wholeness for everyone. So be it!

LEADERSHIP DEVELOPMENT WORKSHOP

Divine Wisdom, guide these leaders who have gathered here today to develop their talents and skills. Thank you for their investment of time and energy to learn more about how they can lead our community to excellence. Thank you for their commitment to the quality of life in our community. Lead them to be wise leaders of others. Guide us all to work together to promote justice, understanding, and cooperation in our community. Show us specific ways to work for the dignity and development of everyone. Amen.

ROTARY CLUB YOUTH CITIZENSHIP
AWARDS BANQUET

Giver of All, we come celebrating your abundant gifts to us. Thank you for the gifts you have given these young people gathered here tonight. We are indeed grateful for their dedication to developing the talents you have given them and to using them in altruistic service to needy people throughout our community. May these young people dare to dream big dreams of changing our world for the better. Help them never to accept artificial limitations that society may place on them, limits based on gender, race, class, or physical ability. Help them to ignore any messages they may receive that restrict their possibilities. Give them courage to hold on to their big dreams that others may call unrealistic or even impossible. May they dream dreams worthy of their best efforts, dreams that will heal and liberate and empower others. Divine Wisdom, guide them as they use whatever power and education they gain to uplift others. Bless them as they make their dreams reality. Amen.

BUSINESS DINNER PARTY

Spirit of joy and laughter, we celebrate your presence here with us this evening. We rejoice in your coming into our lives in familiar and in unexpected ways. We see you in the beauty of creation; we feel you in caring relationships with co-workers and with family; we are often surprised when you come to us through change and new ideas. Continue to open our minds to your creative work within and among us. We ask your blessings on this gathering, with gratitude for good food and fun and time together. May this celebration nurture our partnership with you and with one another as we strive to reach our individual and collective potential. Amen.

ENDNOTES

1. Martin Luther King Jr., "Letter from Birmingham Jail" (April 16, 1963), in *Why We Can't Wait* (New York: Penguin Books, 1964), 77.

2. Martin Luther King Jr., *Strength to Love* (New York: Harper & Row, 1963), 54.

3. Jann Aldredge-Clanton, *Inclusive Hymns for Liberating Christians* (Austin: Eakin Press, 2006), 121.

4. Ibid., 125.

5. Ibid., 138.

Inclusive Blessings and Prayers for Healthcare Settings

MEDICAL CENTER CHAPEL DEDICATION

Gracious Giver of all good gifts, how grateful we are for the gift of this sacred place of beauty and healing. We rejoice as we dedicate this chapel to your glory and goodness. We're indeed grateful for those who had the vision of this chapel, for those who gave generously to make the vision a reality, and for the skills of the architect and builders. [Give thanks for specific individuals or groups, if so desired.]

Bless this holy place and all who come here. May the beauty and holiness of this sanctuary remind those who come weighed down with pain and suffering that you are here with them, renewing and restoring, creating and recreating. Give them grace for the present and renewed hope for the future.

For those who come here too weak and weary to pray, be the Holy Spirit making intercession for them and their loved ones.

For those who feel lost and lonely, be the Shepherd who finds them and carries them in tender arms of love.

For those who feel confused and overwhelmed, come as Divine Wisdom showing them the way.

For those whose hearts ache with grief, be the Loving Mother who comforts them as a mother comforts her children.

For those who come frightened and anxious, bring your Peace that surpasses human understanding.

Rejoice with those who come with gratitude for your healing power.

Dearest Friend through joy and sorrow, we dedicate this chapel to you for your loving care of all those who come here. Bless this chapel for the opening of minds and hearts to new possibilities and revelations.

Come, Thou from whom all blessings flow;
Wake us to see more than we know.
Come, Spirit who makes all things new;
Show us your wider, fuller view.
Give us your visions now to see.
Stir us to be all we can be[1]
Now and forever.

BLESSING OF HANDS

(for people in the healing professions)

INTRODUCTION

Leader 1: We've come together today to celebrate the work of healers. We come to bless the healing work of our hands. Each of us brings unique gifts and a unique self to our various tasks. Today we come to celebrate our call and gifts and to remember how much we need one another. No one person has all the gifts. We rely on one another and work together in this community to bring healing to people who come to us. Through blessing our hands, we acknowledge that they are holy hands, given to fulfill divine purposes. This blessing symbolizes our belief in the sacredness of our everyday lives and work. Through this blessing we recognize the divine presence with us here and now.

RESPONSIVE PRAYER

Leader 2: Spirit of Wisdom, we come seeking you for the work of healing you have given our hands to do. Thank you for working through our hands to provide healing.

All: Healer and Sustainer, we thank you for the privilege of joining hands with those in pain and suffering, of walking with them at the very heart of their lives.

Leader 1: Help us to remember that by our presence, our words, and our actions, we offer to others your life, your hope, and your love.

All: You have given us hands to touch one another's lives with comfort and healing.

Leader 2: Help us never to use our hands to push away those whom we need, nor those who need us.

All: Help us to reach for you in our moments of calm and frustration, anxiety and peace, grief and joy.

Leader 1: May we use our gifts to bring healing to those whom you place in our care.

All: Bless our hearts and hands, Holy Wisdom, and guide us to use them to make whole what is broken in our world.

Blessing and Anointing of Hands

Leaders: We invite everyone who would like to come now and receive a blessing of your hands. We invite healthcare workers in all fields. We all work together to bring healing. (Using water or oil, leaders anoint the hands of each person who comes to receive a blessing. Leaders may softly speak a sentence blessing for each person, such as "May Divine Wisdom bless the healing work of your hands.")

Closing Prayer (in unison)

All: Divine Wisdom, Spirit of love and grace and healing, may we feel your deepest blessing on the work of our hands. May your power within and among us bring healing to all the people we touch. Bless our gifts as we continue to become all you created us to be in your divine image, now and always.

BLESSING FOR INTERFAITH
HEALING SERVICE

Loving Creator, who comforts us as a mother comforts her children, we pray for all those who need your tender care. For all those struggling with illness, some with dying, we ask your sustaining grace and hope. May they feel you with them on their healing journey, understanding their pain and hurting with them. You know each one intimately, for you created each of them with special gifts and purpose. Help them as they search for meaning in the midst of suffering. For all the families of those with illness, we ask your gentle strength and patience. When they feel helpless and overwhelmed, may they know that they are not alone.

Divine Wisdom, guide all those in the healing professions; give us your compassion as we minister to patients and their families. Grant us your understanding love for the hurting people we care for every day. We all come to you as healers and as those in need of healing. Touch us with your comfort that heals our wounds. Give us your grace at the point of our deepest needs. Strengthen us for our healing mission. Touch us with your hope that restores our souls, now and forever. Amen.

BLESSINGS OF STEM CELLS
AND MARROW

(These blessings are for patients with malignant diseases—such as leukemia, lymphoma, Hodgkin's disease, multiple myeloma—who receive stem cell or marrow transplants to "rescue" their immune systems after high dose chemotherapy. The transplant may be from the patient's own cells or from a donor, either related or unrelated.)

BLESSING OF THE GIFT OF STEM CELLS (FROM PATIENT)

For [Patient's name]

Leader: We come today to celebrate a new beginning.
Any new beginning stirs up many feelings within us.

All: We feel afraid and anxious about the unknown,
But at the same time we feel excited and hopeful
as we look forward to new possibilities.

Leader: The cells we bless today, [patient's name], offer new possibilities for your healing. These cells from your own body are an amazing gift from the Creator of all life.

All: Thank you, Mother-Father Creator, for this gift of life and for this transplant as a means of using this gift for healing.

Leader: Loving Creator, our understanding Friend, we thank you for these cells. We bring all our hopes to you as we bless these cells for [name of patient]'s healing.

[Patient's name]: Today I receive these cells with profound gratitude and hope.

Caregivers: [Patient's name], may you feel our hope and love supporting you, bringing you renewed energy and hope.

Leader: May Divine Love and Wisdom be "healing for your flesh" and "marrow to your bones" (Proverbs 3:8 KJV). Spirit of all love and grace and healing, bless these cells for [name of patient]'s healing according to [her/his] deepest needs of body, mind, and spirit. May [patient's name] feel your power flowing through every cell, bringing a new day of health and joy and creative energy.

All: Loving Creator and Friend, come with us now on our journey into the new. Lead us forward with your vision of abundant life, and help us to continue to become all you created us to be in your divine image, now and forever.

BLESSING OF THE GIFT OF STEM CELLS (FROM DONOR)

For [Patient's name]

Leader: We come today to celebrate a new beginning.
Any new beginning stirs up many feelings within us.

All: We feel afraid and anxious about the unknown,
but at the same time we feel excited and hopeful
as we look forward to new possibilities.

Leader: The cells we bless today, [patient's name], offer new possibilities for your healing. These cells are an amazing gift from the Creator of all life and a generous gift from your donor.

All: Thank you, Mother-Father Creator, for this gift of life and for this transplant as a means of using this gift for healing.

Leader: Loving Creator, our understanding Friend, we thank you for these cells. We bring all our hopes to you as we bless these cells for [name of patient]'s healing.

[Patient's name]: Today I receive these cells with profound gratitude and hope.

Caregivers: [Patient's name], may you feel our hope and love supporting you, bringing you renewed energy and hope.

Leader: May Divine Love and Wisdom be "healing for your flesh" and "marrow to your bones" (Proverbs 3:8 KJV). Spirit of all love and grace and healing, bless these cells for [name of patient]'s healing according to [his/her] deepest needs of body, mind and spirit. May [patient's name] feel your healing power flowing through every cell, bringing a new day of health and joy and creative energy.

All: Loving Creator and Friend, come with us now on our journey into the new. Lead us forward with your vision of abundant life, and help us to continue to become all you created us to be in your divine image, now and forever.

BLESSING OF THE GIFT OF MARROW (FROM DONOR)

For [Patient's name]

Leader: We come to celebrate a new beginning.
We come to bless a marvelous gift.
Any new beginning stirs up many feelings within us.

All: We feel afraid and anxious about the unknown,
but at the same time we feel excited and hopeful
as we look forward to new possibilities.

Leader: The marrow we bless, [patient's name], offers new possibilities for your healing. This marrow is an amazing gift from the Creator of all life, and a generous gift from your donor.

All: Thank you, Mother-Father Creator, for this gift of life and for this transplant as a means of using this gift for healing.

Leader: Loving Creator, our understanding Friend, we come bringing all our fears and hopes to you as we bless this marrow for [name of patient]'s healing.

[Patient's name]: I receive this marrow with profound gratitude and hope. I come bringing all my feelings, for "while I kept silent, my bones wasted away in my groaning all day long. For day and night your hand was heavy upon me; my marrow dried up as in a summer draught" (Psalm 32:3–4 MLB).

Caregivers: [Patient's name], may you feel our love surrounding you and nurturing you, bringing you renewed energy and hope.

Leader: May Divine Love and Wisdom be "healing for your flesh" and "marrow to your bones" (Proverbs 3:8 KJV). Spirit of all love and grace and healing, bless this marrow that [patient's name] will receive for [her/his] healing according to [her/his] deepest needs of body, mind, and spirit. May [patient's name] feel your healing power flowing through every cell, bringing a new day of health and joy and creative energy.

[**Patient's name**]: "My lips will praise you, I will bless you as long as I live; I will lift up my hands and call on your name. My soul is feasted as with marrow and fat, and my mouth praises you with joyful lips, when I think of you upon my bed, and meditate on you in the watches of the night; for you have been my help, and in the shadow of your wings I sing for joy. My soul clings to you; your right hand upholds me" (Psalm 63:3–8 KJV).

Caregivers: Maker of all life, Comforting Friend, we praise you. "For you have done wonderful things, plans formed of old, faithful and sure. . . . For you have been a refuge to the poor, a refuge to the needy in their distress, a shelter from the storm and a shade from the heat." You "make for all peoples a feast of rich food, . . . of rich food filled with marrow." You "wipe away the tears from all faces" (Isaiah 25:1, 4, 6, 8).

All: Loving Creator and Friend, come with us now on our journey into the new. Lead us forward with your vision of abundant life, and help us to continue to become all you created us to be in your divine image, now and forever.

OVARIAN CANCER SURVIVORSHIP
CELEBRATION

Holy Wisdom, we come celebrating your presence with and within us as we celebrate ovarian cancer survivors. We come seeking your guidance as we join together to advocate for better means of detecting, preventing, and curing ovarian cancer. Lead us as we work to increase awareness of ovarian cancer and to increase resources for the prevention, treatment, and cure of ovarian cancer. Guide us as we join together in our hope and efforts so that one day there will be no more ovarian cancer. We also gather today in honor of all those women and their families who have experienced ovarian cancer. We celebrate those who have overcome obstacles of illness and those currently meeting the challenges of treatment. Give them hope and healing according to their deepest needs of body, mind, and spirit. We celebrate the strength of spirit of these women here today who have chosen to use ovarian cancer as a door to new friendships and new purpose. We celebrate the courage and hope they find through sharing their stories with one another. Divine Wisdom, guide those who are giving care to women with ovarian cancer and those doing research to prevent and cure ovarian cancer. Bring renewed hope and healing and inspiration through our celebration today. May we be open to new visions and possibilities as we continue to become all you created us to be in your divine image. Amen.

TEAL TEA

*(Teal is the color for celebrating ovarian cancer survivors
and for increasing awareness of ovarian cancer)*

Gracious Giver of all gifts, we come today in gratitude for your gifts of this celebration and all these amazing women gathered here. We celebrate the hope, purpose, and courage these women and family members have found in the midst of the challenges of ovarian cancer. We celebrate the vision, leadership, and generosity of all those involved in organizing this Teal Tea to increase awareness of ovarian cancer and support for its prevention, treatment, and cure. We celebrate the dedication and compassion of those giving care to women with ovarian cancer and those doing research to find a cure. We celebrate all those who support ovarian cancer research. Today we honor women and their families who experience ovarian cancer. May this Teal Tea bless everyone here and nourish our life-giving relationships with one another. May we find increased hope and vision to imagine a world where there will be no more ovarian cancer. Amen

BREAST CANCER SURVIVORSHIP
CELEBRATION

Loving Creator, who gave birth to us all, we come with gratitude for your presence with us. We gather here today to celebrate breast cancer survivors and to join together in our hope and efforts so that one day there will be no more breast cancer. We come today in honor of all those women and their families who have experienced breast cancer. Give them grace and healing according to their deepest needs of body, mind, and spirit. We celebrate the courage and hope that women with breast cancer find in sharing their stories with one another. Divine Wisdom, guide those working to prevent breast cancer, those giving care to women with breast cancer, and those doing research to find a cure. We thank you for their gifts of knowledge, skill, and compassion. We pray for your blessings upon this celebration today, that it will increase hope, understanding, and inspiration. Continue to open our minds and hearts to new possibilities as we continue to become all you created us to be in your divine image. Amen.

WOMEN CANCER SURVIVORS
CELEBRATION LUNCHEON

Our Mother Creator, who gave birth to us all, we gather today in celebration. We come celebrating women—all women, created in your divine image. We celebrate those women who have overcome obstacles of illness. We celebrate those women currently meeting the challenges of cancer treatment. Today we also celebrate those women who give generously of themselves to support other women with cancer. We celebrate women and men healers who give care to women with cancer. We celebrate women and men researchers who work diligently to prevent and cure cancer. Holy Wisdom, guide them as they use their gifts of knowledge, skill, and compassion. For this food and for all the ways you nourish us physically, emotionally, and spiritually, we are indeed grateful. Holy Wisdom, continue to open our minds and hearts to new visions of healing.

> Come, Thou from whom all blessings flow;
> Wake us to see more than we know.
> Help us claim all our gifts and power.
> Fill us with grace that we may flower.[2]

PROSTATE CANCER SURVIVORSHIP CELEBRATION

Gracious Giver, we come with gratitude for your gifts to us. Today we gather to celebrate prostate cancer survivors and to join our efforts so that one day there will be no more prostate cancer. May we feel the power that comes from connecting with one another as we work toward common goals. We come today in honor of all those men and their families who have experienced prostate cancer. Give them healing according to their deepest needs and continued courage as they meet the challenges of prostate cancer. Guide all those giving treatment to men with prostate cancer, those working to prevent prostate cancer, and those doing research to find a cure. For this opportunity to come here today to gain new insights and support, we are grateful. Challenge us to become partners with one another and with you as we strive for health and wholeness. Inspire us with new visions as we seek to become all you created us to be in your divine image. Amen.

MEN CANCER SURVIVORS
CELEBRATION LUNCHEON

Loving Creator, we come together today to celebrate your abundant gifts to us. We come celebrating those men who have overcome the obstacles of illness. We come celebrating all those men who are currently meeting the challenges of cancer treatment. We celebrate those men who give generously of their time and energy to support other men with cancer. We celebrate men and women healers who give care to men with cancer. We celebrate men and women researchers who work diligently to prevent and cure cancer. All of us come here today as healers and as those in need of healing. For your gifts of grace and hope to meet our needs, we are indeed grateful. For your gifts of good food and the opportunity to come together today to gain new insights for health and wholeness, we are also grateful. Source of All Wisdom, open our minds and hearts to new discoveries through this meeting today. Amen

OPENING MEDITATION, WRITING
FOR WELLNESS GROUP

(for patients, their families, and/or medical staff in a journaling group)

Find as relaxed a position as you can where you are sitting, keeping your back straight, your legs uncrossed, and your feet flat on the floor. Close your eyes, and begin focusing on your breathing. Take a few deep breaths, in and out. Breathe slowly and deeply, feeling the gentle rhythm of your breath, feeling your lungs expanding to receive the air and contracting to release it. As you exhale, let go of tension, worry, and stress.

Continue focusing on your breathing, breathing in and breathing out . . . breathing in the breath of life . . . and breathing out tension and stress . . . breathing in the breath of life . . . and breathing out tension and stress. Let your breathing come evenly and deeply and slowly. Breathing in and breathing out, you are feeling more and more relaxed each time you breathe.

As the stillness deepens within you, let your mind slow its pace, adjusting its rhythm to the tempo of your breathing . . . bringing stillness and peace to your inner being . . . letting distracting thoughts that come—and they will—float away like balloons carried aloft by gentle breezes . . . feeling the beauty of the inner world that beckons you deeper and deeper into the center of your being, where the Creative Spirit dwells.

(Pause)

As you continue breathing in and breathing out . . . slowly and deeply and fully . . . in your imagination go to a place where you feel relaxed and inspired. It may be a favorite place in nature: deep in the woods or on a sandy beach or high up on a mountain. Or it may be a place in your own home or backyard, or a place that you create and furnish with the aid of your imagination. Look around at the surroundings, relishing the lovely colors and shapes. Listen to the sounds, or enjoy the silence of this place. Breathe in the peace and beauty surrounding you, feeling yourself becoming more and more relaxed.

Breathing in and breathing out . . . slowly and deeply and fully . . . imagine your breath traveling down your arms to your hands and fingers. These are the fingers that will take memories and images deep within you and will bring them to life on paper. Breathe in gratitude for your fingers and for the rest of your body and for your creative imagination. Breathe in the power of the Creative Spirit within you . . . breathe out distractions and stress. Breathe in creative energy . . . breathe out any distractions. Breathing in and breathing out . . . slowly and deeply and fully . . . you are becoming more open to your feelings and your imagination.

(Pause)

As you continue breathing in and breathing out, your whole being is relaxing and opening to release the Creative Spirit within you. When you are ready, begin to return to this room and the community of people who have come together to write and share our stories.

TRANSPLANT SURVIVORS REUNION

(for patients receiving organ transplants in treatment of liver, heart, lung, or kidney diseases and for those receiving stem cell or marrow transplants in treatment of some malignant diseases)

Gracious Creator, we come today celebrating your amazing gifts of creation and healing. For the splendor and variety of your creation, we are grateful. For this joyful gathering in celebration of life-giving transplants, we are indeed grateful. For the gifts of medical science and wisdom and compassion that have made transplants possible, we are grateful. For the courage and perseverance and faith of everyone who has received a transplant, we are grateful. For the kindness and diligence and patience of all those who have given care so vital to transplant survivors, we are grateful. Loving Creator, we are grateful for everyone here today in partnership with one another and with you in the healing process. Bless this reunion as we celebrate the miracle of life. Divine Wisdom, guide us as we savor each moment of your precious gift of life. May we continue to open our lives to new possibilities and discoveries as we continue to become all you created us to be in your divine image, now and always.

REPRODUCTIVE HEALTH CENTER REUNION

(for parents and their children conceived through In Vitro Fertilization or other assisted reproductive technology procedures)

Source of All Knowledge and Wisdom, we come today celebrating your marvelous work in our world. We celebrate your guidance of researchers who have discovered innovative ways to make new life possible and of health care professionals who have implemented them. You have directed all these advances in medical science, and we are indeed grateful. For the success of this Center for Reproductive Health that brings hope and new life to so many, we are grateful. Bless all these parents and children gathered here today with your love and grace as they grow together. May we all continue to grow toward all you created us to be in your divine image. Amen.

MEDICAL TREATMENT
AND RESEARCH CENTER DEDICATION

Gracious Giver of all life, we gather here today in celebration. We celebrate the generous gifts that made possible this [name the new center for treatment and research]. We dedicate this Center to the healing and health of people now and in the future. We come celebrating the vision, perseverance, energy, and generosity of the donor/s who made this Center a reality. Thank you for these gifts and all other valuable contributions to healing, wellness, total care, and nurturing of body, mind, and spirit. We pray your blessings on this innovative Center for patient care and research. May all the treatment and research conducted here bring healing and hope to many people now and for generations to come. Give us all renewed inspiration and energy to use the gifts you have given us to bring wholeness and fullness of life. Source of all Wisdom, continue to open our minds and hearts to new discoveries for healing as we join together in your goodness and power. Amen.

BREAST IMAGING CENTER DEDICATION

Gracious Giver of every good gift, we gather today to celebrate your Spirit within and among us. For your Spirit of generosity in the hearts of those who contributed to this Breast Imaging Center, we are grateful. For your Spirit of Wisdom in the minds of those who developed imaging technology for the prevention of disease, we are grateful. For the skill and dedication of those who will use these gifts to save women's lives, we are grateful. We come now to dedicate this Center for the prevention of life-threatening disease and for the enhancement of all human life. We dedicate this Center to you and to all our mothers, sisters, aunts, grandmothers, and daughters—all created in your own image. May this Center be used to ensure long, healthy lives. Challenge us to join hands with you and with one another as we continue to strive for health and wholeness for all creation. So be it!

MEDICAL CENTER NEO-NATAL UNIT
DEDICATION

Loving Mother-Father, who gave birth to us all, we ask for your presence and blessings today as we celebrate new life and new opportunities here at [name of medical center]. How grateful we are for this neo-natal unit with all its potential for nurturing your tiniest creations. Bless your little ones who come here and their families. Divine Wisdom, guide the physicians, nurses, and therapists who care for them. Empower all those who take part in this ministry of healing, through your love and grace. Amen.

INTERFAITH PRAYER GARDEN OR CHAPEL DONOR LUNCHEON

Gracious Maker of us all, we're grateful for your vision that draws us here today—
> your vision of healing,
> of beauty,
> of diversity of spiritual experience,
> of connection between spirituality and healing.

We're grateful for our diverse cultural, ethnic, and religious traditions that enrich us and the patients we serve in this medical center. For the gifts and generosity of everyone gathered here, we are indeed grateful. Thank you for this food and for all the ways you nurture our bodies, minds, and spirits. Holy Wisdom, guide us as we work together to bring the [name of garden or chapel] from dream into reality. May the [name of garden or chapel] be a beautiful, peaceful place where patients, their families, staff, and visitors of all faiths can come for meditation and prayer. So be it!

REMEMBRANCE SERVICE

(for people in the healing professions to grieve their losses)

CALL TO PRAYER AND REMEMBRANCE

Leader: We have come together today to remember those we have cared for and have lost. We come to remember patients and their families. We come to remember our own family members and our friends who have passed away. We come to remember these individuals and their gifts to us, the ways they have blessed our lives. Your presence here today demonstrates how deeply you care for people. You have freely given and received love through your physical, emotional, and spiritual care of people. We come today to acknowledge the reality that when we lose someone we love, we hurt. We grieve. So we gather today also to receive comfort from our loving Creator and from one another as we share the pain of loss. Our Creator, who shares our grief, gives us words of comfort through the prophet Isaiah: "Thus says the [One] who created you, [the One] who formed you. . . . 'Do not fear, for I have redeemed you; I have called you by name, you are mine. When you pass through the waters, I will be with you; and through the rivers, they shall not overwhelm you; when you walk through fire, you shall not be burned, and the flame shall not consume you. . . . As a mother comforts her child, so I will comfort you; you shall be comforted'" (Isaiah 43:1–2; 66:13).

PRAYER FOR COMFORT AND PEACE

Leader: Loving Creator, who comforts us as a mother comforts her children, we come to you today for comfort and peace as we grieve our losses. We believe that you understand and feel with us the pain of separation, of saying goodbye. We come to remember and to celebrate the lives of those we have cared for and have lost. We feel profound gratitude for their gifts and graces, and the ways they used them to enrich our lives. We're grateful that they are now experiencing the fullness of your love and healing, free from pain and suffering, exploring in greater depths the beauty and mystery of your creation, experiencing a wholeness and blessedness and peace far beyond our comprehension. Bless us as we fulfill our calling as healers and as we continue to become all you created us to be in your divine image. Amen.

RESPONSIVE PRAYER

Leader: Loving Mother-Father of us all, you gather us close to you. Your arms have gathered many of our patients and loved ones for everlasting peace and nurture and joy.
You hold them close in your love.

All: Guide us as we help those still in our care who are in need of healing and peace and nurture.
May we open our arms of caring.

Leader: You invite us to come to you as we mourn our losses. Your arms offer a warm place, a home of love and comfort in our grief.

All: May we always return to you, to feel your gentle touch and your peace.

Leader: We feel your comfort as you hold us close; we feel your love.

All: May we in turn offer comfort to one another, holding close those who mourn, so they too will feel your love.

Leader: Creative Spirit, you renew our spirits; with you we can soar. You give us hope and strength.

All: May we in turn give hope and strength to others.
May our strong arms uphold others so that together
we may soar unafraid.

Leader: Loving Mother-Father, who gave birth to us all, you rejoice with us at the birth of children; you weep with us when we stand grieving beside a grave. Come among us today as we remember those whom we have loved and lost. We give thanks for them. Help us to continue to grow as healers in your divine image, now and always.

PERSONAL BLESSINGS

(Participants, who so desire, take a rose or several roses laid out on a table in the center of the room. As they hold the rose/s, they name a person or persons they've lost and state gifts from the person/s, or simply hold the rose/s in silence for a moment, and then place the rose/s in one of the vases on the table.)

RESPONSIVE POEM/PRAYER

Group 1: Like a Mother with her children, you will comfort us each day,
giving guidance on our journey, as we seek to find our way.
When we walk through fiery trials, you will help us
take a stand;
when we pass through troubled waters, you hold out
your tender hand.

Group 2: In your image you have made us, calling each of us by name,
giving strength for every challenge as our gifts we fully claim.
We can hear you gently saying, "Do not worry, do not fear;
for I'll always go beside you; every moment I am near."

All: With your vision you inspire us, giving each a holy call;
we will open doors of healing by your power in us all.
Life abundant spreads before us as with eagle's wings
we soar;
joining in your new creation, we rejoice forevermore.[3]

GUIDED MEDITATION (READ BY THE LEADER)

Find as relaxed a position as you can, keeping your back straight and your legs uncrossed. Close your eyes, and begin taking deep breaths. Breathe deeply and slowly in and out. Continue to be aware of your breathing, breathing in the breath of life . . . and breathing out tension and stress . . . breathing in the breath of life . . . and breathing out tension and stress . . . feeling more and more relaxed each time you breathe. Let your breathing come evenly and deeply and slowly. Breathe in . . . and breathe out . . . slowly and deeply and fully . . . breathing out all of your tension and stress.

As the stillness deepens within you, let your mind slow its pace, adjusting its rhythm to the tempo of your breathing. Let your concerns and problems float away like balloons carried aloft by gentle breezes . . . feeling the soft beauty of the inner world that beckons you deeper and deeper into the center of your being, where the Comforting Spirit dwells.

(Pause for several minutes.)

Continue focusing on your breathing . . . breathing in . . . and breathing out . . . slowly and deeply and fully. Imagine the Comforting Spirit with you and within you. Let your imagination suggest images of this Comforting Spirit. It may be an image of a comforting person or something in nature or a strain of music. You are becoming more and more open to the presence of this Comforting Spirit with and within you . . . filling you with peace and grace . . . relieving your grief and pain . . . bringing healing according to your deepest needs of body, mind, and spirit.

Breathe in the healing of the Comforting Spirit . . . breathing in peace and comfort . . . breathing out grief and pain. Breathe in peace. Breathe out distress. Breathe in healing. Breathe out pain. Feel the deep love of the Comforting Spirit flowing through every cell of your body, bringing peace and healing.

(Pause for a few minutes.)

As you feel ready, gently bring yourself back to this room and the company of others who have shared your grief and your hope, refreshed in body and soul by your experience of deep relaxation and the healing presence of the Comforting Spirit.

Labyrinth Meditation (read by the leader)

(If there is an outdoor or indoor labyrinth nearby, participants, who so desire, use it to engage in a walking meditation. Otherwise, provide finger labyrinths for participants who so desire; you can find finger labyrinths to copy free online.[4])

The labyrinth, or prayer path, is a divine symbol found in various religious traditions around the world. The labyrinth is for people of all faiths and people of no particular faith tradition. It has only one path that leads to the center and back out. There are no dead ends. It's not a maze that you can get lost in. It is a single circular path that winds into the center. There is no "right" or "wrong" way to journey on the labyrinth. The path winds around and can become a mirror for where we are in our lives; it touches our sorrows and releases our joys. Take your journey on the labyrinth with an open mind and an open heart.

You may want to pause at the entrance, and become quiet and centered. Open your heart to the journey ahead of you. Become aware of your breath. You may offer a prayer or intention for the journey you are about to make.

Then move purposefully into the center. Observe your process. Moving around the design to the center of the labyrinth is a time for releasing, for letting go of grief and pain and worries in your life. This is a time for quieting your mind, being present to your body, and surrendering to the Spirit.

As you reach the center, you may find your heart opening. Stay as long as you need. The center is a place of meditation, prayer, and illumination. Open yourself to receive the comfort and healing and everything that is there for you.

When you are ready, move back out—back to your life, now refreshed and empowered to live with renewed hope. As you move on the path back out, take the gifts and insights received from the center and integrate them into your whole being.

As you are moving in and out, be aware of your breath. Allow yourself to find the pace you want to go. If you are walking the labyrinth, you may pass people or let others step around you at the turns. The path is two-way; those going in will meet those coming out. Do what feels natural when this happens. Each time you journey on the labyrinth, whether walking or moving your finger, you become more empowered and aware of the Spirit within you.

NURSING EXCELLENCE CELEBRATION

Spirit of all Wisdom and Healing, give us renewed inspiration and power to use the gifts you have given us. We celebrate the healing gifts of the nurses we honor today: [names of those being honored for nursing excellence]. Bless these nurses we are honoring for their excellence in the use of their healing gifts of knowledge, skill, and compassion. May they continue to strive to become all you created them to be. May their feelings of accomplishment spark new dreams and goals. Thank you for families, teachers, supervisors, and all those who contributed to the achievements we have celebrated today. Guide us to chart an excellent healthcare system for the future, one in which all people receive the best possible care. Challenge us all to go forward with new resolve to use our gifts and talents to bring hope and healing, in your loving name. Amen.

MEDICAL SCHOOL GRADUATES
CELEBRATION DINNER

Gracious Giver of all life and gifts, we come celebrating your presence within and among us. We celebrate the healing gifts of these we honor tonight. We rejoice in the academic and clinical accomplishments of [names of graduating physicians]. Bless them as they use their gifts of knowledge, skill, wisdom, and compassion to care for those who come to them. We thank you for teachers, supervisors, co-workers, families, and all those who contributed to the achievements we celebrate tonight. For this food and all the ways you nourish us physically, emotionally, and spiritually, we are also grateful. Source of all Wisdom, continue to open our minds and hearts to new possibilities and discoveries. Guide us to take part in creating a healthcare system in which all people receive the best possible medical care. Inspire us as we seek to use our gifts and talents to bring hope and healing, and to become all you created us to be. Amen.

MEDICAL STAFF MEETING

Gracious Creator, strong in your tenderness and gentle in your power, we ask your blessings upon this meeting. Thank you for the intellect, skill, and compassion of those gathered here. It is amazing to know that you created us in your own image with capacities we have only begun to realize. As partners in your continual creation, we meet you as we develop and use medical technology and spiritual resources to bring healing. How grateful we are that we meet you also at the limits of our knowledge and strength. We meet you in the miracle of a newborn baby. We meet you in the eyes of a person dying in peace and faith. We meet you in our feelings of helplessness when there is nothing more we can do. We feel you in the stamina that comes when we are physically exhausted and emotionally drained. We meet you in relationships of trust and care with our colleagues. Grant us a hope and faith that transcend without denying the painful realities that surround us each day. Open our eyes to our individual and collective potential as your ministers of healing and grace. Give us satisfaction from work well done, but challenge to continue striving and stretching toward all you created us to be, now and always. Amen.

MEDICAL CENTER
BOARD OF DIRECTORS MEETING

Gracious Giver of every good and perfect gift, we come with deep gratitude for your abundant gifts to us. For the beauty and diversity of your creation, for the blessings of health, meaningful work, family, friends, and colleagues, we are indeed grateful. For [name of medical center] and for all the ways [name of medical center] ministers to patients and their families, we are grateful. For all those who bring hope and healing, we are indeed grateful. Every day you remind us that you are constantly creating and recreating, healing and restoring. We are amazed and grateful that we can take part in this work. Thank you for calling us all to your ministry of healing. For these trustees gathered here today and all their contributions to your healing ministry, we are grateful. Divine Wisdom, guide them as they lead and support [name of medical center]. Bless them as they meet here today. Continue to open our minds and hearts to new possibilities and visions as we look toward the future. In your holy name we pray. Amen.

MEDICAL SECRETARIES FORUM LUNCHEON

Loving Maker of us all, we come today with gratitude for your abundant gifts to us. For the beauty and bounty of your creation—multicolored seasons, flaming sunsets, gentle rains, and cool breezes—we are grateful. For the warmth and support of relationships with colleagues, friends, and family members, we are grateful. For the blessings of good health and meaningful work, we are grateful. We thank you that we can be part of [name of medical institution], bringing healing to so many people. We rejoice in this gathering today, grateful for the many talents you have given each one here and for their vital contributions to your work of healing. For this meal prepared for us today and for all the ways you care for our needs, we are indeed grateful. Bless everyone here today with your love and grace. May we all be empowered by your Spirit as we continue to grow toward all you created us to be in your divine image. Amen.

MEDICAL CENTER AUXILIARY BOARD MEETING

Divine Wisdom, we ask your presence and guidance for this meeting. We thank you for the compassion and commitment of those gathered here today. For the variety of gifts that they generously contribute to your ministries of healing, we are indeed grateful. We celebrate their dedicated service given to support the care of people in illness and pain. May this gathering bring new insight, creativity, and energy through relationships with colleagues. Inspire these auxiliary members with new visions of their individual and collective power as your instruments of healing and grace. Give all of us satisfaction from work well done, and challenge to continue striving toward all you created us to be. In your holy name we pray. Amen.

MEDICAL CENTER VOLUNTEER CELEBRATION

Loving and Generous Friend, we come today with gratitude for volunteers who generously give of their talents and time to bring healing to others. We rejoice in your Spirit of love and compassion within them, inspiring them to care for hurting people. Whether through a word of encouragement to an anxious patient, a caring touch to a distressed loved one, a cup of coffee to an exhausted family member, a hopeful word in a support group, or office work for busy employees, these volunteers reveal your loving Spirit. We celebrate the valuable contributions they make through their service at [name of medical institution]. We pray your deepest blessings upon their healing ministry. Bless this celebration today. May we feel the power that comes from connecting with one another as we work toward common goals of health and healing. Amen.

ENDNOTES

1. Jann Aldredge-Clanton, *Inclusive Hymns for Liberating Christians* (Austin: Eakin Press, 2006), 138.

2. Ibid.

3. This litany is from the original version of the hymn text, "Like a Mother with Her Children," published in Aldredge-Clanton, *Inclusive Hymns for Liberating Christians*, 76. An altered version of the hymn is now also in *Celebrating Grace Hymnal* (Macon, GA: Celebrating Grace, Inc., 2010).

4. "Images for Finger Labyrinths." Online: http://www.google.com/images?q =finger+labyrinths&oe=utf-8&rls=org.mozilla:en-US:official&client=firefox -a&um=1&ie=UTF-8&source=univ&ei=jfw.

Inclusive Blessings and Prayers for Faith Community Settings

MARRIAGE/UNION CEREMONY

(This blessing can be used in various parts
of marriage/union ceremonies.)

[Names of partners], it is with great joy that I take part in this blessing of the covenant you are making with each other. This covenant is also a call for you to build together a relationship that makes the world a better place. As equal partners in the divine image, you have the marvelous opportunity to take part in continual creation. You come together to create something new—a new relationship, a new family. Your families of origin will continue to love and encourage you, but you are creating a new relationship. As you grow together, you will support and encourage each other to continue to become all you're created to be. For your sacred journey together, I pray for you many gifts.

[Names of partners], I pray for you the gifts of mutual respect and freedom to continue to develop your talents and to fulfill your callings. Because your relationship is based on mutual love and trust, each of you has enough mental and emotional freedom to remain an individual. May you continue to have the courage to stand as yourself alone and strong so that together you may understand the power of your union.

[Names of partners], I pray for you the gifts of peace and wisdom. May you continue to discover through your commitment to each other a transforming and abiding peace. This peace not only enriches your lives but also makes a difference in our world. May your relationship be guided by Wisdom, and you will spread peace and be happy and blessed, as we read in the book of Proverbs:

Happy are those who find wisdom, and those who get understanding, for her income is better than silver, and her
revenue better than gold. She is more precious than jewels,
and nothing you desire can compare with her. Long life is
in her right hand; in her left hand are riches and honor. Her
ways are ways of pleasantness, and all her paths are peace.
She is a tree of life to those who lay hold of her; those who
hold her fast are called happy (3:13–18).

For your journey together, I also pray the gifts of love and
joy. As we read in the book of Colossians, "Above all, clothe
yourselves with love, which binds everything together in perfect
harmony" (3:14). The deepest intimacy comes from your participation in this divine Love. As you grow together in Love, you
will live out the qualities we find in 1 Corinthians 13: patience,
kindness, humility, rejoicing in each others' accomplishments,
faith, endurance, and hope. (Names of partners), as you have
individually blessed and delighted your families and friends and
so many other people throughout your lives, may you together
continue to share with others the fullness of your joy. Continue
to be filled with gratitude, wonder, humor, and fun that spill over
to all those around you. In the words of the prophet Isaiah, "You
shall go out in joy, and be led back in peace; the mountains and
the hills before you shall burst into song, and all the trees of the
field shall clap their hands" (55:12).

May your partnership be blessed with these gifts and many
more, now and always.

Loving Creator, our Friend, Wisdom, Mother, Father, Sister,
Brother, and so much more than we can name or imagine, we
celebrate your presence with us on this sacred occasion and
ask your deepest blessings on the covenant [names of partners]
are making with each other. We rejoice that you brought them
together through your divine love and wisdom. May [names of
partners] feel your blessing of them as individuals with unique
gifts and your blessing of their loving relationship. As family and

friends, we join in your blessing of [names of partners]. We ask for them a full life—a life rich in meaning, in caring, and in joy. May they continue to drink deeply of your miracles of life and love as they grow together. May their love be an instrument of peace and joy and hope, now and always. Amen.

MARRIAGE/UNION RENEWAL

(This blessing can be used in marriage/union renewal ceremonies
for one or many couples together.)

We come to you, Giver of all good gifts, rejoicing in the gift of loving relationships. Thank you for bringing [give names of partners, if blessing is for only one couple, or say "these couples" if blessing is for more than one couple] together, for all that their [relationship has/relationships have] meant in the past and for what [it/they] will continue to become. We celebrate this time of renewal and recommitment. Help [names of partners (if one couple)/these couples] to grow more and more in their love and respect for each other, encouraging each other to continue to develop their gifts and to become all you created them to be. As they grow in relationship to each other, help them to grow in relationship to you. Bless them as they renew their promises to live in harmony and love. May [this partnership/these partnerships] be instruments of your grace and peace, now and always. So be it!

REHEARSAL DINNER FOR MARRIAGE/UNION

Our Mother-Father Creator, thank you for creating [names of partners] and for bringing them together. Tonight we come to celebrate their love and commitment to each other. We rejoice and delight in them as unique individuals and in their loving relationship. Thank you for this joyful occasion and for everyone gathered here to give blessing and support to [names of partners]. We ask your deepest blessings on their relationship as they continue to grow in love, in joy, and in wisdom. Thank you for this food and for all the ways you nurture us. Bless our celebration this evening and all of us as we continue to become all you created us to be in your divine image. Amen.

BABY DEDICATION

Responsive Blessing

Leader: We gather today for a sacred and joyous occasion. We come to celebrate the gift of creation. In the beginning the Creative Spirit gave birth to the whole universe and all living beings. The Spirit's Hebrew name is *Ruah*. She gave her blessing to all she had birthed, saying, "You are good!"[1]

All: Ruah gave birth to human beings. Ruah created male and female in the divine image. And she gave us her blessing, saying, "Indeed, you are very good!"[2] From the beginning, we have been blessed. Our Creator blessed us when she birthed us.

Leader: The prophet Isaiah reveals that our Creator is like a mother who not only gives birth to children, but who also comforts and nurtures them.[3] Our Creator is also like a father who has compassion for his children.[4] Today we come to praise our Mother-Father Creator as we rejoice in the birth of [name of baby]. We gather to celebrate the blessing that our Creator has already placed upon [name of baby], created in the divine image with creative gifts beyond our imagining.

All: As family both by blood and by faith, we gather to celebrate the blessing of [name of baby] and to covenant to do all in our power to nurture [name of baby] toward all [she/he] is created to be. In doing so, we affirm that [name of baby] is not a gift to us, but a gift living among us. We do not possess [name of baby], but simply rejoice in [his/her] presence among us.

Leader: Creation continually happens. New creation always surprises us, bringing us blessing and hope beyond our expectations.

All: We celebrate the new creation in our midst. We see the miracle of creation here with us today in the form of this precious baby.

Leader: This tiny creation mirrors the divine image. We are amazed as we behold the sacred image in [name of baby].

All: As we give you our blessing, [name of baby], we rejoice in the blessing and hope your very being brings us.

Leader: [Name of baby], we join together now to celebrate and bless your birth.

All: [Name of baby], we rejoice that you are here! Your birth is a great blessing to us all. We thank the Spirit who created you, and we affirm our faith that this same Creative Spirit lives within you. We offer to surround you with steadfast, unconditional love. We promise to give you the mental, emotional, and spiritual freedom to become the individual you were created to be.

Leader: [Name/s of parent/s or guardian/s], we offer our blessing and support to you as you nurture [name of baby].

All: [Name/s of parent/s or guardian/s], we rejoice with you in the birth of [name of baby]! We share your excitement! We offer our support to you as you nurture [name of baby].

Parent/s or guardian/s: With gratitude we accept your blessing and support. [Name of baby], your birth brings [me/us] great joy! [We/I] rejoice that you have come to live in [our/my] home. You are a great gift, but not one for [me/us] to possess. You are in the divine image. The Creative Spirit lives in you. [We/I] promise to give you the mental, emotional, and spiritual freedom to become the individual you were created to be.

Leader: Our Mother-Father Creator, we are amazed that we are created in your own image. Today we are especially grateful for your wonderful creation of [name of baby]. Grant that [she/he] may grow into the fullness of all you created [her/him] to be. May your Spirit of compassion and peace be with [him/her] always. We thank you for this family gathered here today to affirm their love and care for [name of baby]. Guide and strengthen [name/s of parent/s or guardian/s], so that by loving care and wisdom they may nurture [name of baby].

PERSONAL WORDS OF BLESSING

(Participants take turns giving blessings to the baby and parent/s or guardian/s. These blessings can take a variety of forms, depending on the faith traditions of the parent/s or guardian/s and the individuals giving the blessings. Some may perform blessings by placing water on the baby's head, as in baptismal rituals in many traditions. Others may simply place hands of blessing on the baby's head. A small gift may accompany the blessing. Each individual may speak a blessing over the child, choosing among the following blessings or any other blessings he or she wants to give.)

[Name of baby], I bless you in the name of Holy Ruah, our Creator.

[Name of baby], I bless you in the name of our Mother-Father Creator, Redeemer, and Comforter.

[Name of baby], may the One who blessed you with creation continually bless you as you grow toward your fullness in the divine image.

[Name of baby], I celebrate your creation in the divine image and promise to affirm your growth toward your full potential.

[Name of baby], may the Creative Spirit who lives within you nurture and guide you as you develop your creative gifts.

[Name of baby], you have my fullest blessing and my solemn promise to give you affirmation and freedom to become all you are created to be.

[Name of baby], may the Spirit who gave birth to you and who lives within you empower your creative growth as long as you live.

[Name of baby], I affirm the blessing our Mother-Father Creator has already placed upon you and promise to support you as you grow toward all you were created to be in the divine image.

Closing Blessing

All: Holy Ruah, Creator of us all, we come to you with awe as we celebrate the miracle of creation in our midst. Today we feel a special sense of gratitude for your creation of [name of baby]. [She/He] is an amazing creation in your own image. We rejoice in the blessing you have already placed upon [name of baby] when you created [her/him]. We know that you live within [her/him], and thus [she/he] has creative potential beyond our imagining. Give us wisdom and grace never to stifle, but to affirm the gifts you have given [him/her]. May we join you in helping [him/her] grow into the fullness of all you created [him/her] to be, now and always. So be it!

MEMORIAL SERVICE

(These prayers can be used in various parts of memorial services.)

CALL TO PRAYER AND REMEMBRANCE

Welcome in the hope of our Loving Creator, who said, "See, I am making all things new" (Revelation 21:5). We have come together today to celebrate the life of [person's name]. We come to remember [her/his] abundant gifts and graces, and the way [she/he] used them to bless our lives. Your presence here today gives witness to the love [he/she] freely gave and to the love you gave [him/her]. We also gather to receive comfort from our Creator and from one another as we share the pain of loss. Our Creator, who knows our deepest sorrows and is acquainted with our grief, gives us words of comfort through the prophet Isaiah:

> Thus says the [One] who created you, [the One] who formed you. . . . "Do not fear, for I have redeemed you; I have called you by name, you are mine. When you pass through the waters, I will be with you; and through the rivers, they shall not overwhelm you; when you walk through fire, you shall not be burned, and the flame shall not consume you.
>
> As a mother comforts her child, so I will comfort you; you shall be comforted" (Isaiah 43:1–2; 66:13).

PASTORAL PRAYER

Loving Mother, who gave birth to us and who comforts us as a mother comforts her children, we come to you today for comfort and grace as we grieve the loss of [person's name]. We cry out to you in our woundedness. We believe that you understand and feel with us the pain of separation, of saying goodbye to [person's name].

We thank you for giving us tears to express that pain that lies deeper than words. But even as our hearts ache with grief, we celebrate the life of [person's name]. We feel profound gratitude for [his/her] many gifts and graces, and the way [he/she] used them to enrich our lives. Thank you for [her/his] kindness, compassion, determination, creativity, intelligence, wit, sense of life as a precious gift to be lived fully and joyously, and generous spirit that reached out in love to those around [her/him] even as [she/he] struggled with illness [change or add other gifts of this person]. We feel inspired as we remember [his/her] deep love for [his/her] family and friends and all the ways [he/she] brightened their lives. We rejoice in the difference [she/he] made in our world through [name some of the person's specific accomplishments and contributions].

We're grateful that [person's name] is now experiencing the fullness of your love and healing, exploring in greater depths the beauty and mystery of your creation, enjoying a new life filled with new adventures, experiencing a wholeness and blessedness and peace far beyond our comprehension.

Now we pray your comfort and loving care for all the loved ones of [person's name]: for [names of those closest to the person], for other family members, and for [her/his] dear friends. Give us all renewed faith in that day when you "will wipe away every tear from [our] eyes, and death shall be no more, neither shall there be mourning nor crying nor pain any more" (Revelation 21:4 RSV). Amen.

CLOSING PRAYERS

Gracious Maker of all life, we thank you that life, not death, has the final word. We come now not to close the book on the life of [person's name], but to celebrate the beginning of a new chapter, a chapter filled with more blessing and joy and wholeness than we can imagine. We thank you for all the gifts we've received from [person's name] and for those that will continue to flow from [her/his] life. We feel inspired by [his/her] example of strength, courage, determination, generosity, creativity, faith, and love [change or add to this list]. We know that you created [person's name] in your own image with wisdom and creative purpose beyond our comprehension. We rejoice that this purpose does not end with [her/his] too short earthly life, but continues on a larger, fuller scale in the new dimension of life [she/he] has now entered. Hold [names of those closest to the person] and all those who love [person's name] in your arms of love and comfort. How grateful we are that love is eternal, that [name of person's] love for [his/her] family and friends will never die, and that our love for [him/her] will never die. We're grateful that nothing can ever separate us from your infinite love. May we go forth surrounded by this love and filled with new hope of abundant, everlasting life.

Gracious Giver of all life, we thank you for the gift of the life of [person's name]. We rejoice that [she/he] drew deeply from your love and gave deeply of your love. Now we thank you that for [person's name] pain is over, death has ended, and [he/she] has entered a new dimension of life where [he/she] is experiencing love, joy, beauty, and peace far beyond all that we can imagine. Comfort [family members' names] and all the friends of [person's name] with the assurance that [person's name] is more alive than ever before, experiencing the truth of your words in the book of Revelation: "Behold, I make all things new" (21:5 KJV). Amen.

LAY MINISTERS DEDICATION

O Caring One, thank you for your work in the women and men whom we come to bless today. Empower them as we bless their generous volunteer ministry in this community of faith and beyond. We celebrate their gifts and graces as coming from you to be nurtured and gratefully employed by us. May they be instruments of grace and healing wherever you call them. May they be good stewards of this sacred responsibility, and may they experience the deep rewards of being your faithful ministers. As they are fulfilling their call within our community, help them to see the eternal significance even of those tasks that seem mundane and routine. Grant them insight and courage to challenge our community toward new visions. Help them to see beyond what is to what can be. In the midst of a broken world, help them to accept with humility and awe this invitation to be your ministers of reconciling love. Send them forth as bearers of hope and dignity to people who have been dehumanized. Send them forth as bold advocates for those caught in oppressive systems. Send them forth with hope in the midst of futility. Give them now the absolute assurance that they have been touched by you so that they may touch others with your wholeness and peace and joy, through your gracious Spirit. Amen.

PRAISE DANCE PERFORMANCE

Creative Spirit, who lives with and within us, we come today in celebration of your abundant gifts. For the splendor and variety of your creation, we are grateful. For your gifts of music and dance, we are indeed grateful. We marvel that you created us in your own image, giving us your creativity and joy. We pray your blessings on those who have come to praise you today with their gifts of dance and music. Holy Wisdom, guide them as they use these creative gifts to praise you and to bring us visions of your beauty. May every movement and sound they make lift our spirits. Bring delight and inspiration to all of us as we praise you today. Creative Spirit, Holy Wisdom, Source of all gifts, we rejoice in you, now and always. So be it.

DENOMINATIONAL ANNUAL CONFERENCE OR CONVENTION

Rock of Ages and Creator of all things new, we come seeking your stability in the midst of change and your transformation of outworn traditions and crippling attitudes. We come today with many longings, many conflicts, and great hope. We long to be your faithful followers, incarnating your grace and love to needy people in our rapidly changing world. But we must confess our preference for comfort and conformity, and our resistance to risk and change. We too often reach out only to people like us or to those who can benefit us, while neglecting the ones who need us most. Forgive us for our fearful hesitation to follow you wherever your Love might lead us. Help us to follow your example of preaching good news to the poor, healing the brokenhearted, and setting at liberty those who are oppressed. May we see our changing world not as obstacle, but as opportunity for the fresh movement of your Spirit.

Divine Wisdom, grant us understanding of the needs of people today and courage to respond. Keep us from allowing fear, ignorance, or pride to limit the action of your Spirit. Deliver us from customs and prejudices that prevent your creativity within us from bearing fruit. Heal us so that we may be your ministers of healing and transformation. Give us your vision for this conference. Teach us how to be partners with you and with one another in making this vision reality. Guide us in all our business and our worship. Send us forth filled with your power, enthusiastic for your ministry, contagious with your love, and eager to be among your people as ones who serve. So be it!

ORDINATION TO MINISTRY

Leader: Gracious Giver of every good and perfect gift, we gather to celebrate your gifts, especially those gifts of ministry you have given to [name of person being ordained]. We rejoice that you have brought us all here today and that you have been at work for many years preparing the way for this sacred hour. You have gone before [person's name] to break down barriers, open doors, and uniquely equip [her/him] for the ministry to which you have called [her/him]. May [person's name] feel your blessing and power upon [him/her] as we give [him/her] our blessing. May [she/he] feel the peace that comes from answering your call to ministry and the challenge of this sacred responsibility. May [she/he] feel empowered by the blessing of this community of faith. Give [person's name] the absolute assurance that [he/she] has been touched by you so that [he/she] may go forth to touch others with your love and hope and healing. Through this worship service may we all renew our commitments to be faithful to your call to be instruments of peace and grace, now and always.

Congregation: We come to renew our commitments to be instruments of peace and grace, now and always.

Leader: "I will take my stand to watch, and station myself on the tower, and look forth to see what [God] will say to me, and what I will answer concerning my complaint. And [God] answered me, 'Write the vision; make it plain upon tablets, so that [a runner] may read it. For still the vision awaits its time; it hastens to the end; it will not lie. If it seems slow, wait for it; it will sure come; it will not delay'" (Habakkuk 2:1-3 RSV). Let us make plain the vision.

Congregation: What is this vision?

Leader: It is a vision of wholeness and unity. It is a yearning toward the time when the gifts of all are celebrated and nurtured and expressed within faith communities. The vision is of the breaking down of walls that divide us and that prevent us from becoming all we are created to be. In the vision, the men will not say to the women, "I have no need of you" (1 Corinthians 12:21). And the women will not say to the men, "I have no need of you." One faith community will not say to another, "I have no need of you." Instead there will be oneness and mutuality in all relationships. Can you affirm this vision?

Congregation: We affirm the vision and commit ourselves to its realization.

Leader: Gracious Giver of all gifts, we come today with deep gratitude for the gifts and vision you have given [name of the person being ordained]. We come to affirm the blessing you have already placed upon [person's name]. For you have given [person's name] gifts for ministry and have ordained [her/him] to use these gifts to bless others. Through this ordination today we affirm that you have ordained [him/her] for ministry in your world. May [she/he] feel your "Yes" at the deepest level of [her/his] being. May [person's name] always be open to your divine power working within [him/her], often in unexpected, miraculous ways. Give [person's name] power to use [his/her] gifts to work for peace and justice, to bring change for the good. Help [him/her] to claim power with, not over, those with whom [he/she] ministers. Loving Spirit, may [person's name] believe that you are working within [her/him] to care for the broken and the needy, to bring reconciliation and peace, to rejoice with those who rejoice, to weep with those who weep. Holy Wisdom, guide [person's name] to minister in ways that use [her/his] gifts to the fullest to meet the deepest needs of those [she/he] finds wherever you call [her/him] to go. May [his/her] mind and heart be open to struggle with [his/her] own questions and those of others. May [person's name] always be open to new revelations and to new ways of experiencing you as [she/he] continues to become all you created [her/him] to be as your minister. Amen.

ADVENT OF WISDOM

Leader: "Advent" means "coming of something awaited or momentous." This "coming" is not a one-time event. It is a continual awakening, a continual opening to Divine Mystery, a continual growing into all we are created to be.

Group 1: Come now, O Wisdom, we need your clear voice;
Speak and awaken our hearts to rejoice.

Group 2: Gracious Creator of more than we know,
In your own image may we ever grow.

Leader: The news these days reveals a world in need of Wisdom. Children throughout the world are suffering and dying because of war, poverty, and abuse. Women, men, and children suffer oppression and discrimination because of race, gender, class, and religion. We need what the ancient Israelites called *Hokmah* (Wisdom), creative and healing power.

Group 1: Come now, O Wisdom, abide in our souls;
Stir in us visions of life free and whole.

Group 2: Wisdom, our pathway to justice and peace,
With you our dreams find their fullest release.

Leader: We need the continual coming of Wisdom.
"Happy are those who find Wisdom, and those who get understanding, for her income is better than silver, and her revenue better than gold. She is more precious than jewels, and nothing you desire can compare with her. . . . Her ways are ways of pleasantness, and all her paths are peace" (Proverbs 3:13–15, 17).

All: Wisdom, more precious than rubies or gold,
With you our graces forever unfold.
No fame or fortune with you can compare;
Pour out your blessings so rich and so rare.

Leader: Holy Wisdom, continue to come with news of great joy for all people and peace for all the earth. Continue to come to us with fresh power and hope and visions. Guide us to be your ministers of hope and healing for hurting people. Guide us to be prophets for the poor and oppressed. Guide us to support and nurture the gifts of everyone.

All: Wisdom, your grace joins all heaven and earth,
With you we labor new life to give birth.
Come now, O Wisdom, our Midwife and Friend,
Open our hearts to your world without end.[5]

BEGINNING AN INCLUSIVE
FAITH COMMUNITY

OPENING PRAYER

All: Creative Spirit, inspire us as we begin a new community of faith. We come believing that you are working within and among us to create this new community. So we join now as partners with one another and with you as we begin this community. Divine Wisdom, guide our words and actions as we come together to worship and to work for peace and justice.

BLESSING LITANY

Group 1: Any new beginning stirs up many feelings within us. We feel excited as we anticipate something new. But at the same time we feel anxious about the unknown.

Group 2: Beginning is the process of bringing something new into being. Through beginning we become co-creators with the Creative Spirit, who in the beginning created the universe.

Group 1: Beginning takes faith: faith in ourselves and faith in our connection with the Creative Spirit. Believing that the Source of all things is at work within us, we overcome our fear and begin. No matter how small our first step or how timid our beginning, the very act of beginning something new is powerful.

All: We long for a new inclusive faith community.
We hunger for the fresh word.
We thirst for the new experience.

Group 2: We begin this community because we long for the new;
new words speak to our spirits;
new forms empower our actions.

All: The Creative Spirit invites us to begin a new kind of community,

> a community of equals,
> a community of justice,
> a community of creative spiritual growth.

Group 1: In this new faith community women and men of all colors, abilities, and sexual orientations share equally in opportunities and blessings. In this new community all have equal value, and all share equally in leadership and ministry. This new faith community gives sacred value to feminine divinity as well as to masculine divinity.

Group 2: This new community gives equal value to female and male by calling God "she" and "he," "Mother" and "Father," "Sister" and "Brother."

All: We have begun this community;

> we are beginning this community;
> we shall begin this community.

Creative Spirit, our Sister and Brother, we claim your power! May our hopes for new life take wing on your wisdom and your love. For we are your body, your life in our world today. So be it!

MOTHER'S DAY CELEBRATION
(based on Genesis 1)

Leader: In the beginning our Divine Mother gave birth to the universe.

All: She gave birth to light. And she said, "That's good!"

Leader: God gave birth to the earth, and she saw that it was good.

All: She gave birth to the grass and trees and plants of all kinds and said, "That's good!"

Leader: Our Mother gave birth to all the fish, both large and small, that swim in the oceans and to all the winged birds that fly above the earth. And she said, "They are good!"

All: God gave birth to the cattle and to all kinds of animals, and she saw how good they are.

Leader: Then our Divine Mother gave birth to female and male human beings. And she blessed female and male human beings with responsibility for the earth and all the other living beings that she had birthed.

All: We come to celebrate all these gifts from our Divine Mother.

Leader: We come to learn again what it means to be entrusted with these gifts.

All: We join together with our Mother and with one another in giving birth to beauty, peace, and kindness. We join her and one another in nurturing the earth and all living beings.

Leader: Our Mother gives all of us power to give birth and to nurture life.

All: God, our Mother, you continually give life to us. Nourish us and teach us to become all you created us to be in your divine image. Help us to receive your power and love so that others may draw life from us. May we join you in giving birth to new life and in nurturing creation. So be it!

CALLS TO WORSHIP

Woman: Sister Spirit, holy and strong, we hear your voice within calling, "Come to me! There is life in my words and healing in my touch." We come rejoicing that we embody your divine power. Stir our creativity to new life and freedom. Inspire us with fresh visions of wholeness and justice and peace. Guide us with divine wisdom. Fill us with overflowing beauty and compassion.

Man: Brother Spirit, through many languages and cultures, we hear your voice of reconciliation, calling into question and transforming old and discredited notions of power, domination, and control. Thank you for your freeing vision of loving kindness, of strength through vulnerability, and healing through openness. Restore and recover a sense of our common humanity as we seek to forever turn up a new leaf at the table, welcoming everyone into your house.

Together: Celebrate the Spirit in all of us and in all creation.

Man: Let us celebrate the sacredness of every living being.

Woman: Let us claim our holy power.

Man: Let us dare to dream big dreams of bringing peace to our community and our world.

Woman: Let us dare to believe that we contribute to healing our global community by gathering here as a faith community to share our visions.

Together: Come to us, Spirit from whom all blessings flow;
Wake us to see more than we know;
Help us claim all our gifts and power;
Fill us with grace that we may flower.[6]

Leader: "I am about to do a new thing;
      now it springs forth, do you not perceive it?
      I will make a way in the wilderness
       and rivers in the desert. . . .
      for I give water in the wilderness,
       rivers in the desert" (Isaiah 43:19–20).

All: We come today expecting a new thing!

Leader: Yes! The Creative Spirit, who gave birth to us,
      calls us to new life,
      to new ways of seeing and being.

All: Today the Spirit invites us to see our community and our world
      not the way they have been,
      nor the way they "have to be,"
      but the way they can be.

Leader: We come today with great expectations!

All: We come with great expectations of new revelations!

How lovely is your dwelling place, O Holy One! Our souls long for your presence. Our hearts sing for joy to you. How lovely is your dwelling place. Blessed are those who dwell in your house, ever singing your praise.[7] Let us rejoice today in this holy place in the Holy Presence.

Now is the time to come alive with joy and thanksgiving! Now is the time to seek and to find the precious treasures of Wisdom as we worship. Now is the time to rejoice and dance with the Spirit of Life. Come, let us celebrate!

~ ~ ~

Leader: Come, let us worship our Mother and Father, the Ground of our being, the Source of our lives, the Spirit who sets us free.

All: To worship is to dance with the Spirit of Love, who is alive in each of us.

Leader: To worship is to open our minds and spirits to new revelations, to hidden truths.

All: Through worship we speak and sing our visions of the new creation into reality.

Leader: Through worship we breathe the air of a time yet to be, a time when barriers are broken down and wounds are healed.

All: Let us celebrate with hope that silenced voices be heard, trembling voices be made strong, oppressed people be set free, so that the Spirit at work yesterday, today, and forever be proclaimed.

~ ~ ~

Leader: Grace to you and peace from our Mother and Father Creator.

All: We celebrate our partnership as sisters and brothers on mission to free and include all voices and all gifts in our faith community.

Leader: The Spirit calls us to wholehearted commitment to this mission.

All: We will move forward side by side, inspired by the Spirit.

Leader: Our mission of inclusiveness is not easy in the time and place in which we live.

All: The Spirit will give us power, even now as we worship.

"Arise, shine; for your light has come" (Isaiah 60:1). Our hearts shall thrill and rejoice. Awake, for the Spirit lives within us! Give thanks to the Holy One, whose "steadfast love is higher than the heavens, and whose faithfulness reaches to the clouds" (Psalm 108:4). Arise! Awake! Rejoice!

Come, let us worship the Great Creative Spirit, who gave birth to all life. Let us rejoice that this Creative Spirit lives in each of us! Let us claim the Spirit's power within and among us. Come, praise the Creative Spirit!

~ ~ ~

Leader: We give thanks, Spirit of Wonder, for the marvel of your creation that surrounds us.

All: We give thanks for all the wonders of life we enjoy.

Leader: We give thanks to you, because you have given us life.

All: You have made us in your image and breathed your breath into us. We are alive with divinity, and your glory is manifest in us. We come praising you!

Leader: Let us see your glory, your justice, and your peace.

All: May our lives and our world be reawakened by the power of your grace, now and always!

~ ~ ~

Leader: "Happy are those who find Wisdom and who get understanding. For her income is better than silver, and her revenue better than gold. She is more precious than jewels, and nothing you desire can compare with her. . . . Her ways are ways of pleasantness, and all her paths are peace. She is a tree of life to those who lay hold of her; those who hold her fast are called happy" (Proverbs 3:13–15, 17–18).

All: We come today seeking Wisdom. If we seek Wisdom, she will come to us. Come, Wisdom! Come to us today!

Leader: Mother-Father Creator, Living Water to all who thirst, in you we "live and move and have our being" (Acts 17:28). Glory and praise to you!

All: When the poor and the needy search for water, and there is none, and our tongues are parched with thirst, then you answer us; you will not abandon us. You make rivers run on barren heights and fountains in the valleys. You turn the wilderness into a lake and dry land into springs of water.[8] We thirst for truth and justice. We come to drink from the flowing fountains of Living Water.

Leader: O sing unto the Creative Spirit a new song! Sing, all the earth! Declare the Spirit's glorious, marvelous works among all the peoples! Sing a new song of praise and glory![9]

All: Celebrate a new heaven and a new earth! For the first heaven and the first earth are passed away. And the Creative Spirit said, "See, I am making all things new" (Revelation 21:5). Come, let us celebrate with thanksgiving!

Leader: Come, let us worship the Life-Giving Spirit. To worship is to exult in the poetry of our faith.

All: To worship is to renew the vision. It is to unloose the bindings and break forth in the freedom of the Spirit.

Leader: The Spirit's vision of making all things new is alive!

All: Let the vision come alive in us!

~ ~ ~

Leader: Let us now begin our worship of the Source of our lives, the Ground of our being, our Mother and Father, the Spirit who sets us free.

All: Now is the time to celebrate! Now is the time to rejoice in the Spirit who empowers us.

Leader: Come, let us celebrate the good work of the Spirit among us, calling for our wholehearted commitment.

All: We commit ourselves anew to this inclusive faith community, working side by side, firm in the Spirit. We come together now in the power of the Spirit!

~ ~ ~

Leader: This is the day that our Creator has made. Let us rejoice and be glad in it.[10]

All: It is good to give thanks, to sing praises to your name, O Most High. It is good to proclaim your steadfast love in the morning, and your faithfulness by night. For you have made us glad; at the works of your hands we sing for joy. How great are your works![11]

Leader: You gather us together in covenant as a hen gathers her brood under her wings.[12]

All: How great is your loving care! We come now to praise you!

~ ~ ~

"Speak out for those who cannot speak, for the rights of all the destitute. Speak out, judge righteously, defend the rights of the poor and needy" (Proverbs 31:8–9). Through our gathering here today, may we find courage and power to speak out for the poor and needy. May Wisdom guide our words and actions.

~ ~ ~

"Let justice roll down like waters, and righteousness like an ever-flowing stream" (Amos 5:24). May our worship not be just lovely words and songs. May it be challenge and inspiration for actions of justice. Come, Divine Wisdom, to guide us!

~ ~ ~

Leader: Why do we come here to worship? Whom do we worship? What is the goal of our worship?

All: We come here to worship the Holy One, who tells us to do justice, to love kindness, and to walk humbly with our Creator.[13] The goal of our worship is to challenge and inspire us to do so. Let it be!

~ ~ ~

Leader: Come, let us sing for joy to our Mother-Father Creator. Let us make a joyful noise to the rock of our salvation. Let us come with thanksgiving and praise. Come, let us worship the One who created the earth and all that is therein.[14]

All: We come to worship our Maker! We come to give thanks and sing for joy!

"Wisdom cries out in the street; in the squares she raises her voice. At the busiest corner she cries out; at the entrance of the city gates she speaks. . . . Prize her highly, and she will exalt you; she will honor you if you embrace her. She will place on your head a fair garland; she will bestow on you a beautiful crown" (Proverbs 1:20–21, 4:8–9). Let us listen to Wisdom's voice today as we worship. Let us prize Wisdom highly and follow her teachings of peace and justice. Come, let us listen to Wisdom and follow her!

INVOCATIONS

We come rejoicing that you guide us, as an eagle stirs up her nest, and hovers over her young; as she spreads her wings, takes them up and bears them on her wings.[15] Mother Eagle, help our talents and imaginations to take wing with you. As we sing and pray and rejoice, fill us with your power and your love. May our spirits soar with you in this time of worship and always!

Loving Maker, thank you for creating us all in your divine image so that we have the wonderful gift of imagination that helps us know you as Mother, Father, Sister, Brother, Lady Wisdom, Shepherd, and so much more. As we worship today, help us to imagine you in many ways so that we may know how great you are and how much value you give each of us. May we feel you within us, among us, and above us. Stir our hearts to rejoice in your amazing love and grace. Amen.

Divine Wisdom, guide us in this time of worship. Inspire us to go with you on your paths of peace. For you are a Tree of Life, and we long to receive your gifts so that our words and our actions will be life-giving. We come today with open hearts and hands to receive your gifts that are more precious than gold. Lead us, Holy Wisdom, in this worship time and every day so that we will be instruments of your peace, love, and kindness in our world. So be it!

O Spirit of Love, may we feel your presence within and among us today as we worship you. Inspire us with your beauty. Fill us with your power. Transform us with your grace. Amen.

Sister-Brother Spirit, who inspires us all,
   come to our gathering here this day,
   as we join together with people of faith,
     past and present, around the world,
     who have overcome and remained faithful
     to the vision you have blazed within them.
Light the fire of your vision within us,
   so that we will be faithful to our calling,
   now and always!

O Spirit of Power, open our lives to your inspiration as we worship today. May we feel you within us and among us as we speak and sing your praises. We rejoice in the splendor and diversity of your creation. Empower us to join your creative work in our world. Give us fresh meaning and purpose as we follow your call. Amen.

Our Glorious Maker and best of all Friends, we come to praise and worship you today. You have created us for communion with you, and our souls are restless until they find rest in you. We know that you are here with us and within us. Help us to open our minds and hearts to all that you have to give us in this time of worship so that we may be instruments of your peace and love in our community and our world. Let it be!

We praise you, Sister-Brother Spirit, for your work within us and among us. Transform us through the power of your love and peace. Stir within our hearts afresh in this worship hour, so that we may join you in healing our wounded world. Come, Sister-Brother Spirit! Come to us today!

Holy Wisdom, who created billions of stars in the universe and people in the world, we are amazed that we are created in your image and that you live within us. As we worship you today, may we all feel how precious we are to you. May each girl and boy, each woman and man, feel the power of being a marvelous creation in your divine image. Open our imaginations more fully to all you are and all you created us to be, now and always.

Loving Mother-Father, who gathers us in the tenderness of your arms, gently lead us in paths of truth as we worship today. Nurture within us a hope that expects goodness, a faith that endures, and a love that transforms us and those around us. Give birth to new life within us. So be it!

In your presence, Creative Spirit, who gave birth to the universe, we stand in wonder. In your presence, we rest in trust. In your presence, Divine Wisdom, we ask for guidance. O Holy One, who includes and exceeds all creation, we celebrate your power and your work within us, even now. Amen.

Creative Spirit, whose bright beauty shines through flowing streams and flaming sunsets, shine your glory into our hearts today. Open our minds to your truth within us, among us, and surrounding us. Open our spirits to your vision of shalom for all creation. So be it!

Eternal Source of Truth and Light, we rejoice that you are in our midst today. Illumine our hearts and minds. Awaken us to the radiant joy and abundance of life in your Spirit. May your presence in this worship time today comfort us and challenge us to open ourselves to new revelations. So be it!

May we feel the presence of the Spirit, who is everywhere, with us now in this time of worship. May we feel the Spirit moving in our hearts to unsettle us and to inspire us. May we be stirred by the Spirit's power within us, among us, and beyond us! Let it be!

Great and Glorious Creator, the whole world is full of your glory! We are filled with wonder and gratitude for the beauty of your creation. How excellent is your name in all the earth! Fill us with your beauty, love, power, and peace, now and always.

Sister-Brother Spirit, we come today needing your peace. Spirit of Power, we come needing your strength and energy. Bread of Life, we come needing your nourishment. Living Water, we come needing your renewal. Spirit within us and among us, stir our hearts today! Let it be!

We come into your presence, Most High and Holy One, with awe and profound gratitude for your great goodness to us. We praise you because you are worthy to receive honor and glory and blessing. We dare to believe that you are already here, waiting to pour out your power and blessings upon us as we worship today. Amen.

Gracious Mother-Father, more loving than any earthly mother or father, we come to you for reassurance and challenge in this hour of worship. Holy Wisdom, we come to you for guidance. Fill us with your Spirit so that our words are your words; our songs, your songs; our thoughts, your thoughts. Help us to know your perfect love and peace more fully so that we will go forth to live out your image in us. So be it!

Infinite Love and Power, inspire us in this time of worship. Wake us to your wonders within and all around us. Open our hearts to new revelations. Challenge us to dream big dreams of ways we can join you in changing our world. Let it be!

Come, Spirit of Love. Fill us with your grace and power this day. Bring us comfort to go through our pain and sorrow, courage to attempt great things for you, and faith to expect great things from you. Come now, Spirit of Love!

Life-Giving Spirit, we know that you are here, waiting for us. By your love, you conceived us. By your care, you nurture us. By your sustaining grace, you hold us. Feed us with the Bread of Life today, that we may go forth nourished and strengthened to feed others. Let it be.

Holy Wisdom, time and again throughout history you have anointed your prophets and sent them on your mission to speak your good news to the poor, to heal the sick, to free the captives. You have always been renewing the earth in such a variety of ways that creation sings of your glory and the human family reflects your beauty in a thousand different ways! We pray that through the power of your Spirit you will anoint and send us on your mission. In this time of worship may we join together as sisters and brothers to receive your guidance and power. So be it!

Loving Mother and Father, Brother and Sister, Wisdom and Healer, Friend and Guide, and far more than we can name or imagine, we celebrate your presence with us today and throughout our lives. By your power, you have led us. With your grace, you have nurtured us. We rejoice in your absolute, everlasting love. May our celebration today result in renewed commitment to you. Help us to catch a glimpse of your vision of peace and wholeness for our world and to join you in making the vision reality. Excite us with new possibilities! Challenge us to dream big dreams! So be it!

Maker of All, create new life in us today as we worship. Awaken us to new revelations and new possibilities. Transform us with your love and power and hope so that we may be your peacemakers in our community and in our world. Amen.

Holy One, we come to glorify you and to celebrate your presence with us. You are far beyond our highest thoughts, yet you live within us. How amazing! We come today with awe and expectancy. Your gracious presence is with us day and night. But we set aside this time of worship to increase our awareness and appreciation of your presence. Satisfy the deepest longings of our hearts and send us forth with renewed courage and power. So be it!

We celebrate your presence within us and among us, Loving Spirit. Thank you for giving us encouragement and hope for all of life. Help us to feel a special sense of your presence in this worship time. Open our minds and hearts to your truth today. Fill us with gratitude that overflows to others who need your loving care. Amen.

PRAYERS OF THE PEOPLE/PASTORAL PRAYERS

(Read names of people in the congregation who have asked for prayer and who have given permission for their names to be read in the worship service.)

Loving Creator, our Mother and Father who gave life to us, gather us now in your strong and tender arms as we bring our joys and concerns and longings to you. We join in prayer for all those just named and for others who need your care. With those celebrating new life or renewed health or other good news, we give thanks. With those who are weary or hurting or grieving, we ask for rest and relief and comfort. Give us all grace according to our deepest needs of body, mind, and spirit.

We come believing that you are also our Loving Friend through joy and sorrow, walking beside us and giving us strength for every day and every need. But often we don't feel you with us. In the midst of pain and conflict and frustration, we often wonder where you are. Our hearts cry out for help.

When our strength and patience fail, you often surprise us by coming through a call from a caring friend, through a note of encouragement, through the beauty of music or nature, through the laughter of children, through a warm hug. For these gifts, we are grateful. And we are grateful that you come through this community of faith, overflowing with gifts, a warm and welcoming community that down through the years has been a beacon for justice and peace in spite of opposition and obstacles.

May we all continue to join with you and with one another in breaking down barriers of prejudice, injustice, ignorance, and poverty so that Peace can heal our world. May the beauty and holiness of this worship service remind us all that you are constantly creating and recreating, healing and restoring. Holy Wisdom, Hokmah-Sophia, continue to open our minds and hearts to new possibilities and discoveries as we continue to become all you created us to be in your divine image.

Come now, O Wisdom, healing power;
Your grace all earth extols;
Your touch can make our spirits flower;
Your love restores our souls.[16]

Holy One, far greater than our highest thoughts, we come amazed into your presence. How incredible it is that your care reaches each one of us in so many ways. We thank you for the gift of children, for their minds eager to learn, for the ways they teach us about trusting you. We thank you for the dedication and diligence of teachers who give generously of their talents and energy. How grateful we are for the support and care of this community of faith.

Gracious One, we come to you today with our good intentions, our mixed motives, our limited grasp of truth, our half-hearted commitment. We are so grateful that you accept us just as we are, but that you constantly urge us to become so much more. You have created us in your own image with minds and souls to catch a glimpse of your vision for our world. You give us the capacity to dream great dreams. Help us to have the faith to turn these dreams into reality. You know the external and internal obstacles that stand in our way. Some of us face limited financial resources. For some, physical limitations and illness make life such an uphill struggle that little energy is left. We contend with feelings of fear, indifference, and hopelessness that keep us from being your instruments of reconciliation and change. We often resist change, even when we know it is needed. Whatever our limitations and obstacles, fill us with renewed power so that we can empower the powerless. Forgive us when we see human need and walk away, saying that there is nothing we can do about it. Help us to truly believe that we can be part of your miraculous work in our world. Let it be.

O Loving Friend, we celebrate your presence with us. In a world of uncertainty, how grateful we are that we can rely on your faithfulness. How reassuring it is to know that you accept us just as we are and that you love us enough to challenge us to become more than we are. How astounding it is to know that the great Creator of the universe is also our Friend. We long for a closer, more authentic relationship with you. You know all the things that block our simple acceptance of your friendship. The pressures and responsibilities of work and family and finances and school often keep us focused simply on surviving, rather than on enjoying communion with you. Help us to feel you running with us when we must run, and help us to accept times of rest as gifts from you. You know the burdens of grief and guilt that make us depressed and anxious, wondering if anyone really understands or cares. Help us to feel you close to us, as that Friend who bears all our burdens with us. Break through every barrier that keeps us from receiving your unconditional love and acceptance so that we may give love and acceptance to other needy people. May we join your work of healing in our world. Amen.

Loving Mother-Father, who gathers us in the tenderness of your arms, we come today to draw strength from you. We bring our concerns to you because we believe you care for us. Sometimes we forget all the ways you have been with us and helped us, and we need reminding of your concern. For there is no where we can go and no experience we can go through that takes us away from your caring presence. How grateful we are that you hold us in your everlasting arms of love even when we become too discouraged, too indifferent, or too weary to hold on to you. When we feel life crushing down upon us, come to us with your renewing love. Nurture within us a hope that is continuously expectant, a faith that endures, and a love that transforms us and those around us. Create new life within us. Amen.

O Thou who comforts us "as a mother comforts her child" (Isaiah 66:13), we need the comfort of your tender arms around us. We trust that you are ready and waiting to journey with us. But there are times when we lose touch with you and wonder where you are. Our spirits give way, and we cry out in our distress and anguish. Help us to believe that you are close by even when we do not feel your presence. You have promised never to abandon us, never to leave us comfortless. We come claiming your promises, believing that you care for us more than we can feel or imagine. We come in faith that you are on our side, always wanting the best for us. Today we especially ask your comforting care for [names of ill and grieving people in the congregation who have given permission for their names to be read]. May they feel your loving arms around them, giving them grace for the present and hope for the future. We give thanks with those who are celebrating good news: [names of people who have had babies, people who have experienced marriage or holy union, and people recovering from illness who have given permission for their names to be read]. Strengthen us all with your hope and peace. Surround us with your comforting love, now and always. Amen.

O Caring One, we give thanks for your promise never to leave us nor forsake us. But sometimes in the midst of suffering and other challenges, we don't feel you with us. Reassure us that you go with us always and that you care for us more deeply than we can imagine. We come to you, wanting to feel your presence and to know that you are guiding us. We bring all our cares and burdens to you. Go with us through our challenges and sufferings. Bring healing according to our deepest needs of body, mind, and spirit. May your Spirit within us bring grace sufficient for each day and each need. Calm our fears, and bring us peace that surpasses all human understanding. Comfort us in our losses. Hold us in your loving arms. Give us your blessed assurance that you are leading and guiding every step of this healing journey, now and always. Amen.

Mother-Father of the Cosmos, how majestic is your name! We praise you whose compassion touches us in countless ways. We feel you through music, laughter, warm hugs, and forgiving acts. You provide our daily needs as loving mothers and fathers provide for their children. How grateful we are that you are concerned about every aspect of our lives. Help us to see your hand in all the necessary details of our daily lives. But keep us from frittering away our time and energy and talents on unnecessary, insignificant details. Show us specific ways to live out your purpose for our lives.

We come to you today with all our needs and concerns. We especially ask your healing care for [names of ill and grieving people in the congregation who have given permission for their names to be read]. May they feel you with them, giving them peace and comfort. We give thanks with those who celebrate good news: [names of people who have had babies, people who have experienced marriage or holy union, and people recovering from illness who have given permission for their names to be read].

Many times we feel overwhelmed by all that we see to do. Thank you for coming to us in those moments when our strength and patience fail. Give us power to stand up for what is right, to speak out for what is good, and to act for justice. Forgive us when we waste our power through fear or timidity, or when we use it for our own selfish purposes. Help us to use our strength and talents to join your work of love and peace in our world, through your gracious Spirit. Amen.

Gracious Fountain of Every Blessing, we come to you today as people needing to drink from your goodness and grace. We're grateful that you know our needs and hearts' desires. You know our sorrows and our joys. You know the deepest longings of our hearts. May we drink deeply of your blessing of peace that calms our fears. May we drink deeply of your blessing of grace that restores our souls. May we drink deeply of your blessing of love that makes us whole. May we drink deeply of your blessing of hope for our future. Pour out your blessings also on our families and friends who care for us. Nurture them with your abundant blessings. May we all feel your healing and your power flowing through us like streams of life-giving water. With the blessings you have poured out on us, help us to bless others and to bring healing peace to our world. Amen.

"Do not fear, for I have redeemed you; I have called you by name, you are mine. When you pass through the waters, I will be with you; and through the rivers, they shall not overwhelm you; when you walk through fire, you shall not be burned, and the flame shall not consume you" (Isaiah 43:1–2). Thank you, Gracious Creator, for reminding us of your great love for us. How amazing that you know each of us by name and that you go with us through all our challenges. Through our pain and suffering, you go with us, helping us survive. Through our grief and distress, you go with us, giving us hope. When we cannot feel you with us, reassure us with these promises. Renew our faith in your caring presence with us always. Give us your abiding peace. Hold us in your arms of love. With the love and comfort we have received from you, help us to reach out to others in need of your comforting care. Give us all faith that you will be with us, now and forever. Amen.

In the midst of pain and conflict and frustration, we often wonder where you are. We feel your absence more than your presence. We cry out to you in our pain and our loneliness, and we wonder if you hear us and if you care. At times we feel discouraged, even hopeless. Other times we try to steel ourselves against pain by shutting off our feelings. And we become cold toward others and even toward you. Our hearts cry out for answers. But more than answers, we need your presence. We need reassurance that you are working for good within our lives. Like a Mother Eagle, lift us up when we are weak and weary. Bear us up on your strong wings. Carry us when we cannot carry ourselves. Hold on to us even when we cannot hold on to you. Help us to know that you carry us even through experiences we cannot understand, but that you do not leave us completely dependent. Strengthen us as we continue to grow into all you created us to be. Amen.

Our Mother-Father, who gave birth to us all, we come to celebrate our relationship with you and with one another. We come amazed that we are your very own daughters and sons, created in your image, and that you want to relate to us. We rejoice that we feel your love and understanding through the concern and encouragement of brothers and sisters within this community of faith. You strengthen our faith as we learn from one another and minister to one another. We are indeed grateful that within your divine mystery you use our prayers and deeds of kindness as instruments of your healing.

We offer our prayers today for the healing of [names of ill and grieving people in the congregation who have given permission for their names to be read]. Give them and their families peace and strength sufficient for each hour and each day. May they feel assurance that they are in your hands where all is well.

Spirit of Wisdom, we turn to you for direction in the midst of many voices that lay claim to our attention. Help us steer clear of the glitter and glamour with which some people would clothe your message. Others present messages they call "holy" in bland and banal garb. Help us to discern your truth for our times and to follow your paths of peace and love. Through our caring and sharing, may those who are suffering know healing. Forgive us when we let sentimental words and time-honored forms become substitutes for love in action. Show us specific ways we can provide food and shelter for the poor, companionship for the lonely, encouragement for the fearful, hope for the discouraged. Fill us with your Spirit who gives us power to be your love in our community. Amen.

Our most understanding Friend, we rejoice that you go with us through every moment and every experience of our lives. You are the Living Water who quenches our thirst, refreshes our weariness, and soothes our wounds. We thank you for tangible evidence of your care—comfortable places to worship you freely according to the dictates of our conscience, food to nourish our bodies, opportunities to learn. And we thank you for the spiritual renewal you offer as we gather here to worship as a community of faith. How exhilarating it is to remember that you have created us in your own image and that you constantly inspire us to stretch toward our full potential. How comforting it is to know that the Great Maker of the universe cares about each one of us personally and wants the best for us. Guide us as we care for one another in this faith community and in our larger community. Give us compassion for the sick and grieving, the abused children, the unemployed, those in physical and spiritual pain. Show us specific ways that we can reach out with care and kindness.

Caring One, we confess that we don't always want to help others. And sometimes we want to hold on to our prejudices and grudges. We have been quick to accuse and slow to forgive. Sometimes we had rather nurse our wounds than put forth effort to bring healing. Help us to take responsibility for our attitudes and actions. Give us grace to make needed changes in ourselves so that we can join you in bringing change to our world through your peace and power.

Holy Wisdom, we come seeking you today, just as people throughout the ages have sought you. May we be diligent in our searching and open to new revelations. But we must confess that we have often been like those who have rejected and scorned your words of truth and justice. You know what holds each one of us back in our search for you. You know and understand our deepest fears. Some fear disillusionment—that you will let us down as others have. Some fear loss of control. Others fear that you may guide us to change in ways that will be difficult and painful. Depression and loss of hope keep some from believing that the search for you will be rewarded. Others just don't want to learn anything new, even from you. Help us to understand that you want to work in partnership with us, and that joining with you will enable us to be the best we can be. Guide us to go with you on your paths of peace and justice. May we believe that by joining with you we can make a difference in our community and in our world. Let it be.

We come today thirsting for you, Giver of Life. We long for your wellspring of hope. Physical refreshment, like a cool drink of water and air conditioning on a hot summer day, points to the deeper spiritual renewal you offer us. We feel weighed down by all the suffering in the world. Why do millions of women suffer and die from domestic violence? Why do millions of children suffer and die from poverty? Why are millions of children abused every day? Why do millions of people throughout the world suffer from racism, sexism, and heterosexism? Give us hope and wisdom to join you in eliminating the oppression that causes all this suffering.

Our personal struggles and sicknesses and sorrows don't always make sense to us. But we reach out in faith for your presence and strength and meaning. Loving Spirit, give us power and courage to overcome hardships to fulfill your highest intentions for us. Forgive us when we make excuses for not using what we do have and for not getting involved with others in need. Show us ways we can make a difference in easing pain and righting wrongs. Help us to use our voices and votes so that all may have freedom and opportunity to become all we're created to be. So be it.

Source of Life, we celebrate the beauty and wonder of your creation. May we expect your coming to us in life-changing ways this day. How amazing it is that you love us enough to keep inviting and encouraging us over and over again to change, and that you give us power and strength to change. We come to you, Holy Wisdom, believing in you for the guidance and grace we need. We come to tell you of our physical challenges and to ask for healing, courage, and patience in the midst of suffering. We come to tell you of our heartaches, believing that you understand the pain that we can share with no one else. We lay before you the deepest longings of our souls, knowing that in you alone is true fulfillment and peace. We also bring before you the needs of our community, praying that you will help those who suffer from hunger, unemployment, abuse, and injustice. Teach us ways to be part of your solution. We pray for healing and peace in our world. Divine Wisdom, guide the leaders of all nations to make peace on earth a reality. Forgive us when we look at situations and people and pronounce them hopeless. Remind us that you never have and never will give up hope for all the people you have created. May we be partners with you in bringing hope and healing to our community and to our world. Amen.

Eternal Source of Truth and Love, we come longing for you. Sometimes you seem so far above and far away. Are you really concerned about us? The question often haunts us. But yet we have felt your presence in our lives—sometimes in dramatic ways and sometimes through quiet, everyday events and relationships. There's so much we don't know about you. But we find in Scripture many word pictures to help us know and experience you. You are like a strong, comforting Mother and a warm, protective Father, always wanting the best for us. Sometimes we feel you as that stable Rock in the midst of our chaotic, confused, and frustrating days. When we feel at our wit's end, you are that Fortress of strength to hold us together. When we have exhausted all our resources and feel totally helpless to cope with some problem, you come to us as Wisdom and Hope. When we are sick or discouraged, you come to us as Physician and Friend. When we feel overwhelmed in grief, you are our Comforter.

May everyone here today and others in our prayers feel you in ways that meet their deepest needs of body, mind, and spirit. Help us to draw upon your unlimited resources. Forgive us for trying to shrink you into what we can understand and control. Our narrow-mindedness, fear, and pride often keep us from letting you be all you want to be in our lives. Forgive us, and open our minds and hearts to receive more of you so that we have more to give to our needy community and world. May we receive your unconditional, unlimited love so that we may love more fully and freely, beginning even now. So be it.

Sister-Brother Spirit, we rejoice in your power to bring us together in loving community. You guide us to give equal value to everyone—women and men, girls and boys of all races and religions. We celebrate your continual work in our lives and in our world. We rejoice that you live within and among us, bringing meaning, hope, and joy. But sometimes we don't feel like rejoicing. We become overwhelmed and overextended with all our responsibilities. There are those here today who feel the heaviness of grief and pain. Financial burdens weigh others down.

Comforting Spirit, give us a hope and a joy much deeper than any painful realities we are experiencing. Bring healing and comfort to [names of ill and grieving people in the congregation who have given permission for their names to be read]. Show us specific ways we can join you in caring for them. Guide us to reach out to others who are sick, poor, hungry, frightened, or lonely. May we open our hearts and hands even to the most unlovable. Help us to listen to your voice within us, calling us to grow in love and acceptance of others. So be it.

~ ~ ~

Giver of Life, whose love exceeds our deepest longings, for you our souls wait. How grateful we are that there is nowhere we can go away from your Spirit, nothing we can do to separate us from your loving presence. This is the faith that we hold on to, even when we don't see your hand or feel your presence.

We pray that you will touch each one of us at the point of our deepest needs. Touch us with your love that casts out all fear. Touch us with your comfort that heals our wounds. Touch us with your grace that restores our souls. Touch us with your joy that renews our hope. Forgive us when we become trapped by the trivial into neglecting the weightier matters of justice and mercy and love. Deliver us from worshipping forms and symbols instead of the reality for which they stand. Help us never to become so set in our ways and in our ideas that we lose the sense of wonder and expectation in our faith. How grateful we are that you are the Creator of the new—new life, new revelations, new opportunities. We open ourselves to your new creation. Teach us to be partners with you in creating a new world where justice prevails, where love overcomes, and where beauty abounds. Come to us today with your transforming power and your abundant life. Amen.

Birth-Giver, we come to you today with mixed feelings. We are grateful for the blessings in our lives and for the beauty of creation. We are grateful that you care so much for us that you keep challenging us to change and grow. We are grateful for the excitement and hope that come with new possibilities. But we also come honestly before you bringing feelings of fear, anger, doubt, and grief. We fear the loss of security and the uncertainty that come with change. We're angry over the pain and injustice we experience and over all the suffering we see around us. We're filled with doubt as to whether things will get better or worse and whether you really care about us. We grieve our losses through illness and death.

Divine Comforter, we hold on to our faith that you understand all our feelings and feel with us. We pray especially today for those in our community who need your comforting and healing care, for [names of ill and grieving people in the congregation who have given permission for their names to be read]. We pray also for the needs of people in our larger community. Holy Wisdom, guide us to focus on solutions rather than problems. As we see the fresh beauty of your creation, give us faith that you have renewal in store for us. Open our minds and hearts to join your miraculous work in our world. Amen.

≈ ≈ ≈

Our most faithful Friend, we come into your caring presence just now. We know that your love for us is unconditional and ever-lasting. How astounding it is to know that you place immense value upon each one of us. We want to draw deeply from your love today, to learn from you what faithful love is all about. We rejoice that we feel your love through the care and concern of this community of faith. We know that you have brought us together in relationship to share our joys and sorrows and gifts. Teach us to love one another enough to respect and celebrate even our differences. May we as a faith community use our stresses and difficulties to grow in our understanding of one another and of your purpose for our community. Show us ways to care for one another when we are hurting. Today we especially remember [names of ill and grieving people in the congregation who have given permission for their names to be read]. May they feel your healing presence and strength.

Help us all to recognize those parts of our lives that are sick and in need of your healing. Free us from those things that get in the way of our receiving your love. We get impatient and irritated when you don't work on our schedule or give us our way. Forgive us, Gracious Friend, and give us faith that you have a timetable and a way that is best for us. We often block your love by getting frustrated by trivial details and petty misunderstandings. Forgive us, and break down barriers of pride, stubbornness, and indifference, so that your love can flow freely through us. Help us not to hoard the love we receive from you. Open our hearts to unloved people. Help us to remember that your love extends even to the most unlovable people, and that you want to increase our love to include these as well. May we join you in reaching out to others with love and grace. Amen.

"Where can [we] go from your Spirit? Or where can [we] flee from your presence? . . . If [we] take the wings of the morning and settle at the farthest limits of the sea, even there your hand shall lead [us], and your right hand shall hold [us] fast" (Psalm 139:7, 9–10). Loving Mother-Father, how grateful we are that you are with us everywhere and always. But often we don't feel your presence. We sometimes wonder if you lead us or if things just happen at random. All around us we find confusion and chaos. Give us assurance that our lives have meaning and purpose. Remind us that you have plans for us, plans to give us "a future with hope" (Jeremiah 29:11). Renew our spirits with this hope. Show us specific ways we can join in your plan of transforming our community and our world with peace and love. Amen.

Loving Mother-Father, gentle in your power and strong in your tenderness, you have created us in your own image. How astounding! You are Divine Mystery beyond our knowing, yet you care for each one of us. How amazing! We thank you for caring for our physical needs—for clothing, shelter, nourishing food. We pray for those who suffer from physical deprivation. Show us ways that we can help relieve hunger and provide for other physical needs. We are grateful that you care for our emotional and spiritual needs as well. When we feel discouraged and weak, you come with reassurance and strength. How grateful we are for the hope and joy you give us through new babies born into our community of faith. May we help nurture them in your love, and may they be a sign to us of the new life you are birthing in our midst.

Forgive us when we become impatient and fearful because we don't see the evidence of your work that we want to see.

Divine Wisdom, guide us on your mission for our faith community. Keep ever before us your vision of transforming our world through love and peace. Show us concrete ways to turn that vision into reality, and then give us courage, patience, and faith to work with you toward the vision. Help us to be your active, faithful instruments of peace and healing, now and always.

Why have you forgotten us? Where are you? We call out to you with our questions. We feel your absence more than your presence. We cry out to you in our pain and our loneliness and wonder if you are really there. Sometimes life crushes down upon us, and we feel discouraged and hopeless. But then you come to us, Caring Sister-Brother Spirit, through a call from a friend or the hug of a child or an affirming note from a co-worker. Thank you for believing in us even when we don't believe in ourselves.

Caring One, we know you feel the grief that many here today are experiencing. You hurt with us over lost loved ones and shattered dreams. Help us to believe that your love is with us even through times when we don't feel your presence. We confess that we often contribute to the pain and brokenness in our world. We have let small differences mushroom into large difficulties while ignoring what draws us together in love. Help us to change attitudes of resentment into love, and accusation into patient understanding. May we feel your loving acceptance of us so that we reach out to others with your love and grace. May we join you in caring for our sisters and brothers in need. Amen.

Understanding Mother and Father, we need to feel your comforting arms around us. We come as your children needing an encouraging, life-giving word and touch from you. How grateful we are that you come to us in so many ways—through laughter with friends, through unconditional love of family, through shared work within this community of faith. When we have been discouraged or bored, you have often surprised us with unexpected blessings. In times of uncertainty and fear, you have laid your reassuring hand of peace upon us. In times of pain and grief, you have comforted us with your healing hand. Today we pray that your strong, tender hands of healing will be upon [names of ill and grieving people in congregation who have given permission for their names to be read]. We rejoice with [names of people who have had babies, people who have experienced marriage or holy union, and people recovering from illness who have given permission for their names to be read]. Bless us all according to our deepest needs of body, mind, and spirit.

Use our hands, Loving Mother-Father, to bring wholeness to a world torn by strife and divisions. Help us to believe that we can make a difference. If the forces for good seem to have gone into hiding, help us to be among those who still act boldly to bring your peace. Forgive us when we had rather talk about you than let you live in us. Challenge us anew to answer your clear call to join your work of love. Amen.

O Wisdom, beloved One, why are you so far from us? Our world suffers from your absence. Few seek to be faithful to you. Few seek you, even though you cry out to us in a loud voice, "How long, O simple ones, will you love being simple? How long will scoffers delight in their scoffing and fools hate knowledge?" (Proverbs 1:22). We come today seeking you. We need your grace and healing in our personal lives. We want to bring your presence to our community. Show us the way. O Wisdom, come to us! Teach us when to speak and when to be silent. Show us when to be cautious and when to move ahead with your truth. Teach us when and how to confront injustice. Show us how to change those things that diminish your creation. Teach us to speak and act to affirm the worth of all your creation. Guide us on your paths of peace and justice. Give us your vision for our community. Help us to join you in bringing wholeness to all creation. O Wisdom, come to us! So be it!

Gracious Maker of all, we come celebrating your abundant gifts to us. We are grateful for health and strength that enable us to come here today, for opportunities to give and to receive, for the beauty of a sunset and the sparkle in the eyes of children, for music and laughter, for delicious fruits and ice cream. Help us to stop and think about all the things that go right in our lives, instead of focusing on what goes wrong. So many things go right in our work, in our families, in our congregation, in our physical bodies. We especially rejoice in the spiritual gift of your unconditional love. May we feel in the depths of our souls your acceptance, even when pressures and problems and failures make it hard for us to accept ourselves.

Loving Spirit, we open our hearts honestly today. You see the places where we are wounded and broken. You know there are some here whose pain weighs them down, making it hard to feel thankful. We pray your healing for families torn by conflict, for those whose hearts ache with loss, for those who suffer chronic physical illness. We pray today especially for [names of ill and grieving people in the congregation who have given permission for their names to be read]. Help us to respond more fully to the needs of our hurting sisters and brothers in this community and around the world. Forgive us when we make excuses for not reaching out in love. May your love cast out our fears and empower us for ministry. Give us faith to believe that the more we give, the more cause we will have for thanksgiving. May our hearts overflow with gratitude to you now and always. So be it!

In the presence of the Great Creative Spirit who flung the stars into space, we come in awe. In the presence of the Spirit whose breath stirs within us and causes our hearts to thirst for meaning, we come in need. Hear our longings, Loving Spirit. At times we have called to you and heard only silence. May we hear your gentle voice within our spirits and in all of creation. May we recognize you in all the people we encounter.

Gracious Spirit, you live in us and know us fully. You know our hidden hurts and our deepest fears that we don't feel we can share even with those closest to us. You understand our grief that lies deeper than words. Help us to feel your understanding comfort and peace. We ask for wholeness for ourselves and for our community. Free us from prejudice and selfishness that limit your work within us. Guide us toward new steps of faith. May we allow the divine creativity you have placed within us to bear fruit. Give us enthusiasm to reach out with our gifts to minister to those in need. Let it be.

Giver of Abundant Life, we celebrate your presence with us, among us, and beyond us. We are grateful for opportunities within this community of faith to give and to receive, for feelings of accomplishment that come from work well done, for the pleasure of good food and relaxation. But no matter how satisfying these experiences are, we still find ourselves restless and longing for more. How grateful we are for glimpses of a deeper dimension of life, for the spiritual reality that lies within and beyond the activities of our daily lives. We rejoice in the miracle of your love and peace. Awaken us to the beauty of your presence, even in the midst of struggles and problems that threaten to obscure our vision of you.

Divine Healer, come to those here today who are burdened and wounded. Minister to them according to their deepest needs of body, mind, and spirit. Comfort those who grieve the loss of loved ones, loss of jobs, loss of relationships, or other losses. Restore those who suffer from physical and emotional illnesses. Show us ways that we can be your instruments of love and healing to hurting sisters and brothers in our congregation, our community, and around the world. Help us to accept our limitations and to find rest and restoration when we feel weary and burned out. But help us not to use our limitations as excuses to keep from striving toward your ideal. Give us courage to act upon our convictions, and generosity to give freely of ourselves and our resources as an expression of our gratitude for your gifts. Amen.

Eternal Wisdom from whom our wisdom comes, Questioner from whom our questions arise, Lover of whom all our loves are hints, Comforter in whom we find our rest, Mystery in whose depths we find meaning—come to us today in whatever ways we need your presence. We praise you who are beyond all that we can think or imagine, and marvel that you live within each one of us. How amazing! We praise you for renewing our lives with hope that flows through our spirits like a spring of fresh water. We praise you for this community of people who nurture our faith and challenge us to grow. We praise you for caring for our physical, emotional, and spiritual needs.

Compassionate Friend, we bring our needs to you today. We bring our loneliness, asking for assurance of your presence and companionship. We bring our frustrations and failures, asking for peace and confidence in our worth and abilities. We bring our doubts and discouragement, asking for fresh faith and hope. We bring our physical problems, asking for your healing touch and patient strength. Enfold us now in your presence. Restore us with your peace. Renew us through your power. Ground us in your grace, now and always.

How grateful we are that we can come to you, Loving Maker, knowing that you care for us more than we can ever imagine and that you want to give us abundant blessings. Your gifts come in so many forms: warmth and shelter from the cold, the beauty of autumn trees decked in bright yellow and gold and red, loving words of family and friends, meaningful work, relationships within this community of faith. But those here today who are struggling with illness or grief or failure may feel life more as a burden than a blessing. Give us all reassurance that you are with us and for us through all of life. And help us to remember that "weeping may linger for the night, but joy comes with the morning" (Psalm 30:5). Assure us all that fresh blessings await us.

We confess that we often hoard your gifts. We close our ears to the cries of people who are hungry and poor, while focusing only on our own comfort and security. We spend too much of our money and time on things that cannot bring us true happiness. We thank you, Gracious One, that you are always ready to forgive us and to give us new opportunities to live as you intended. Help us to discover the joy of receiving through giving. So be it.

Loving Mother-Father, we come needing your comfort and care. We often wonder if you hear our cries for help. Those who have been suffering with illness a long time may especially be struggling with questions: Are you there? Do you hear our prayers? Do you really care for us? Even in the midst of questions, bring reassurance of your loving presence. Assure us all that you will never leave us nor forsake us. Those who are grappling with fears of failure and doubts about themselves need assurance of their infinite worth. Assure us all that we don't have to be perfect to fulfill your special purposes for us. Forgive us for selling ourselves short and taking the easy way out. We often become too comfortable and set in our ways to do those things that we know will bring us the greatest joy and fulfillment. We often spend too much of our time and money on material things. Forgive us when we hoard your gifts for ourselves. May we continue to discover the joy that comes through generous sharing of the gifts you have given us. Amen.

Maker and Sustainer of Life, we rejoice that your love for us is infinite, beyond all we can think or know. Your concern for us far exceeds our understanding. We pray for deeper understanding, but even more for faith that reaches beyond the limits of our understanding. May we feel the depth of your care for us even in the midst of our heartaches. We come to you today with different needs, but all longing in some way for your healing touch and your words of reassurance. Sometimes we become so tired or sick or discouraged that we cannot even pray. Help us somehow to feel deep within our hearts that you are holding on to us even when we have no more strength to hold on to you. Help us to find some meaning even in our painful experiences of loss and failure and conflict. May we find new hope and strength in this community of faith today. May we see that you have created each one of us for a special purpose, and that we are of great value to you. We confess that we often make excuses for not striving to become all you created us to be. Some may say, "I'm too young to do that," while others say, "I'm too old," or "I don't have enough education," or "I don't have time now," or "I can't do that because I'm a woman or because I'm a man." You know the ways that we pass up opportunities to become all you intended. Forgive us, and help us to resolve today to answer your call to develop our gifts and to use them for good. We thank you for creating us in your divine image and for calling us to join your healing work in our world. Amen.

~ ~ ~

Holy Wisdom, we know that you are here, waiting to give us your blessing. Before we ever thought of trying to find you, you called out to us. You have always been seeking us, longing to give us your peace and wholeness. You are waiting now, not for us to be good enough, but for us just to receive your gifts that are more precious than all the fine jewels in the world. Nothing can compare with you. On your paths of peace we will find life and blessings.[17] We are anxious and empty, in need of you and all you are offering us. You know how we need you to guide our lives. Often we miss your gifts because we fill our lives with constant activity and noise. We seek financial success, entertainment, and material things instead of you. Often we had rather complain about our problems and nurse our wounds than receive the peace and joy that you freely offer us. Help us to hear your words and join you in bringing new creation to birth. Teach us the grace of receiving as well as the grace of giving. As we receive your precious gifts, show us ways to share these gifts with our community and our world. So be it!

~ ~ ~

We praise you, Creative Spirit, for your marvelous gifts to us. You restore our souls with your creation, bursting with beauty. You renew us through meaningful relationships in this community of faith. Through the miracle of your grace, you bring blessing and strength to us as we share your gifts with others. We thank you for this congregation gathered here to draw power from you and from one another so that we may minister to those in need.

Today we come lifting our needs to you, our understanding Friend. You know us better than we know ourselves. We trust you to come to us at the point of our deepest needs. Today we pray your comfort and healing for [names of ill and grieving people in the congregation who have given permission for their names to be read]. We rejoice with [names of people who have had babies, people who have experienced marriage or holy union, and people recovering from illness who have given permission for their names to be read].

Caring Friend, we come to you as people who do not care enough. We mean well, but so much gets in the way of our doing much about the needs of other people. Forgive us for letting trivial things and petty worries trap us and sap the life out of us. Forgive us for thinking more about what we're going to have for dinner or about football scores than about our sisters and brothers here in our community and around the world who suffer from hunger and injustices. We confess that we have not always lived up to our potential, that we have not developed and used all the gifts you have entrusted to us. Help to believe that it is never too late to change. Show us new ways to share the treasure of your gifts with others. Amen.

We come to you, our Loving Mother-Father, with gratitude for your abundant blessings: the freedom to gather here for worship, the beauty of blossoming trees and flowers, the enthusiasm of children, the deep-down assurance that you are with us and for us no matter what. Our hearts go out today to those who are hurting, to [names of ill and grieving people in the congregation who have given permission for their names to be read]. Show them anew how fully you care for them, and restore them according to their deepest needs of body, mind, and spirit. How grateful we are for opportunities to learn and grow. We thank you for the gifts and dedication of teachers who use their wisdom and knowledge to help children and adults stretch toward all we're created to be. Help us to open our minds to your truth, never becoming satisfied with where we are in our understanding or in our service. Guide us to translate our knowledge and beliefs into loving actions. Let it be.

Spirit of Hope and Healing, we come to you with yearning, expectant hearts. You have come into our lives again and again in countless ways. We look forward now to your coming with new revelations and renewed power. Come into the wounded places in each of our lives—those places where we have suffered losses, disappointments, frustrated goals, failure to achieve all we wanted, rejection, or injustice. Come, Great Comforter and Advocate, with your restoration and strength to help us keep striving. Sometimes we call out to you and wonder if you hear us and care about us. Open our hearts to signs of your work in our lives. Open our minds and spirits to receive you in unexpected ways. Come into the sinful places in our lives—the unforgiving attitudes that turn into poisonous resentment, the greed that robs us of the joy of giving, the prejudice that keeps us from receiving the gift of relationships with the rich diversity of people you have created, the doubt that keeps us from great ventures with you. Forgive us, and change us. Help us to look beyond ourselves to the needs of people around us, to those who suffer from illness and poverty. We confess that we often eat so much that our stomachs ache while others ache from hunger and malnutrition. Help us to become more generous in sharing our resources with needy people. May we join you in your work of love and grace in our world. So be it.

Our Loving Maker and Friend, we come this morning recognizing our deep need of you. We know that in you we "live and move and have our being" (Acts 17:28). At the same time you give us freedom of choice. We celebrate this freedom, although some choices are not easy and clear cut. Help us to draw strength and wisdom from you and from one another in this community of faith. May we learn better how to bear one another's burdens. We pray now for those with physical burdens: those living with chronic pain and illness, those suffering from terminal illness, those suffering from addiction to drugs and alcohol. We pray also for those with emotional burdens: those experiencing disappointment and failure, those grieving lost relationships, those living with resentment.

Reach out to us all with your arms of comfort and love. Teach us specific ways to join you in caring for one another. May we also draw hope and healing from the bright signs of new life all around us in your creation. Forgive us when we are too preoccupied or indifferent to appreciate your gifts to us. Forgive us when we are too proud to accept the gift of care from others, and when we become so bogged down in our own problems that we fail to reach out to others with care and concern. May we experience your grace through receiving from one another and through giving to one another. Amen.

Eternal, Infinite Wisdom, we come into your presence knowing that we stand on holy ground. How amazing it is that you want to relate to us. We dare to believe that the great Maker of the universe, who flung billions of stars into space, knows each one of us by name, has even numbered the hairs of our heads, and cares about every detail of our lives. We come to you now as a community of faith, caring for one another. How grateful we are that we can feel your love through this community, that we can share our joys and our sorrows. We rejoice today with [names of people who have had babies, people who have experienced marriage or holy union, and people recovering from illness who have given permission for their names to be read]. We hurt with members of our community who are hurting. Bring your comfort and healing to [names of grieving and ill people in the congregation who have given permission for their names to be read]. And we bring to you today those needs that people feel they cannot share. You know that we are all wounded and limited. Help us to bring even our weaknesses to you to be transformed into instruments of your healing to others. Give us strength for each challenge we face. Help us not to waste our time and energy on trivial and petty things. Open our minds and hearts to the deep meaning and joy of following your paths of peace and justice. So be it.

High and Holy One, how grateful we are that your love extends even to the smallest creation. Your love comes to us in so many forms, at work and on holidays. You come to us through celebrations with family and friends, through times of study and creativity, through quiet times of rest and meditation, through relationships within this community of faith, through reaching beyond this community to help people in need. May we always be open to new and unexpected ways you may come to us. Help us to feel your presence even in the difficult times of our lives. When we are hurting or discouraged or angry, help us to feel you beside us, caring and giving new strength and courage. No matter how you come to us, we are grateful for your coming. In the presence of your love, we feel our deep worth. In the presence of your power, we feel strong and confident. In the presence of your peace, we feel calm reassurance. Your love also inspires us to love all others as our sisters and brothers. Show us how to incarnate your love in the specific opportunities you give us. Give us wisdom to know how to work with people who seek our help. Give us faith to believe that actions that may seem small to us can make a big difference. Give us the courage and energy to carry out our good intentions. Send us forth into our needy world as messengers of peace and love. Let it be.

Sister-Brother Spirit of Life, we come believing that your restoring power is available to us today. We come seeking the new life you continually offer. We have often felt dry and lifeless within, and you have revived us again and again. We pray for your reviving power today. Many in our community of faith need physical restoration. The pains and needs of their bodies are constant, heavy burdens that make it hard for them to feel your presence. Teach us the best ways to share their burdens and to give your loving care to them. You know the struggles that go on within each one of us, struggles between what brings true life and joy and what gives only temporary comfort and pleasure. You know our resistance to doing what we know is right, the inertia that keeps us from the action we resolve.

We say we want to spread your love, but we are often too busy or too greedy to commit ourselves in any costly way. And often we see so much pain and injustice that we don't really know what our response should be. Help us not to take the easy way out by convincing ourselves that because we cannot do everything, we can do nothing. Show us specific actions we can take, and give us faith to believe that in your strength we can make a big difference. Breathe new vitality and courage into us this day. Inspire us so that we become more alive than ever before. May we feel this new life begin to surge through us even now. So be it!

Marvelous Creative Spirit, we praise you for the great things you have done and are doing in our midst. We rejoice that we are in your own image with amazing gifts of creativity. We praise you for your miraculous work within and among us, for your unexpected blessings, for all the gifts you have given us, for the ways we experience you within this faith community. Give us greater sensitivity to the needs of people within and outside this community. Show us ways that we can reach out with your love. May we comfort one another with the assurance of a victorious faith, a faith that turns weeping into joy.

Loving Friend, we ask forgiveness for not trusting in your unconditional acceptance of us and for not giving this acceptance to others because we are often concerned about appearances. Forgive our self-centeredness and closed-mindedness that keep us from ministering to needy people. Give us an urgency for spreading your love so that the dreams you have for the world might be more fully realized in our day. Give us hope and patience for the in-between times, the times of waiting and preparation. Give us wisdom and courage through challenging times of change. Inspire us to proclaim your truth and to join your work of justice and peace. Let it be.

Spirit of Joy, awaken us to your presence within and among us. Revive our spirits. Strengthen our hope. How we need your healing, refreshing springs of life. We come thirsting for you. Some here today cannot feel you because their hearts are heavy with grief. Others feel weighed down with family responsibilities or financial burdens. Others suffer from pain and illness that sap most of their energy. Bring your comfort and restoring power. Even though we have experienced your presence and power in our lives, we all have times when we feel down. Other times we try to steel ourselves against pain by shutting off our feelings.

Faithful Friend, we confess that we have often tried to hide our feelings from you, from this community of faith, and even from ourselves. And many times we have failed to look beyond ourselves to discover hope and healing in you. We have become so preoccupied with our own concerns that we have failed to hear the cries of hurting people near us and around the world.

Forgive our selfishness and our lack of compassion. Help us to use our suffering to bring comfort and encouragement to others. May we join your work of love and peace. So be it.

Most caring Friend, we come to you today with deep gratitude for your faithfulness. We celebrate your work in our lives, bringing physical healing and restoring our spirits when we are discouraged. We thank you for continuing to strengthen our relationships with one another in this faith community. Show us ways to be your arms of comfort and healing to [names of ill and grieving people in the congregation who have given permission for their names to be read]. May they feel your love and know how precious they are to you. We all come to you today in need of your healing touch. Only you can satisfy the deepest longings of our hearts. But so many things seem to get in the way of our relationship to you. The necessary details of our lives, like keeping ourselves and our things running, often sap our time and energy, and we wonder where our days have gone. And then something unexpected happens that shatters our schedules and plans. Help us to feel you even in the midst of mundane details and interruptions. For we know that you are in us and in all things. Wake us up to your presence. Give us your peace that keeps us from being anxious and fearful. Give us your love that lifts us beyond our own concerns to minister in specific ways to hurting people all around us. Give us your hope that keeps our dreams and visions alive, now and always.

Glorious Giver of Life, we come rejoicing in your great goodness to us. We celebrate the beauty and the variety of your gifts to us—of summer and winter, of vacations and meaningful work. How grateful we are that you come to us in the quiet places of our hearts, within this community of believers, and even in the midst of uncertainty and conflict. We gather to worship you because we believe that as we relate to you and to others in this faith community, we grow toward all you created us to be. We come to draw strength from your unconditional love and acceptance. You know our deepest needs and feelings. You go with us in our joys and our sorrows, our moments of exhilaration and of despair. We are grateful that you have given us the capacity to feel deeply, but we know that by loving deeply we open ourselves up to the pain of loss and rejection. Many here today feel the heavy pain of grief that sits like lead on the heart. Help us to feel you hurting with us in the painful times of our lives. Restore hope and purpose. May we use our pain to grow in compassion for others in need and to reach out to them with the comfort we have received from you. Give us the humility to admit that we don't have all the answers, but the certainty of your concern for us.

Forgive us, Gracious Giver, when we waste your gifts. Those of us gifted with sight or hearing often miss the beauty that surrounds us. Gifted with conscience, we become comfortable with sin. Gifted with the power to think, we fall for lies that cater to our ignorance and prejudice. Gifted with imagination, we plod along afraid to dream or create. Forgive our negligence and challenge us anew to use our physical, intellectual, and spiritual gifts to bring joy and peace to ourselves and others. Let it be.

Everlasting Love, who holds the past and present and future in your hands, we praise you for the great things you have done and are doing in our midst. In a world of uncertainty, how grateful we are that we can rely on your constancy. In the midst of change, how grateful we are that your grace and compassion never change. We come rejoicing in your faithfulness to us in our joys and in our sorrows, through times of strength and times of weakness. We know that you are here with us today, sharing all our feelings. You are with those who rejoice, and we also celebrate with [names of people who have had babies, people who have experienced marriage or holy union, and people recovering from illness who have given permission for their names to be read]. You are with those who are hurting and grieving, and we also hurt with [names of ill and grieving people in the congregation who have given permission for their names to be read]. Show us ways to minister to others as you have ministered to us.

Divine Wisdom, help us to be open to your new word beyond our traditions and habits. Guide us on your pathways of peace and justice. Show us ways we need to change ourselves and our community. But you know our mixed feelings about change. We grieve the losses that come with change and fear the uncertainties. But we also feel an expectancy as we await the new opportunities and new blessings you have for us. Give us courage and renewed energy to join you in working for change. Give us grace to embrace your vision of wholeness for our world. Let it be.

Infinite, inexhaustible Creative Spirit, far exceeding our capacity to comprehend or even name, how marvelous it is to know that you want to relate to us as Friend. You feel our deepest joys and sorrows, rejoicing and weeping with us. As a community of faith, we come rejoicing with [names of people who have had babies, people who have experienced marriage or holy union, and people recovering from illness who have given permission for their names to be read]. We celebrate new relationships and restored health. We also come sharing the pain and sorrow of [names of ill and grieving people in the congregation who have given permission for their names to be read]. Surround them with your hope and peace.

We thank you, most Loving Friend, for coming to us in many small, everyday ways—in the touch of a loved one, in the sight of bright blue and red flowers along the highway, in the smell of honeysuckle, in the sound of children at play. And you come to us at times in dramatic ways, lifting us from the concerns of this world into a spiritual dimension of life that we cannot explain. When we have felt the mystery and wonder of relationship with you, we are amazed and changed. In those moments we feel at one with you. But we don't always carry the mystery of those moments with us. We are left not knowing quite what to do with our mystical experiences. We are too quick to forget the wonder and to settle back into our old ways. We too often take the easy way out and just go on about our business as though nothing had happened. Help us to go on in faith that something of eternal significance has happened, that you have come into our lives and want us to continue to change. Show us the specific changes you want each one of us to make to continue to grow in your wisdom and love. Let it be.

Loving Maker of us all, how grateful we are that you have made us in your divine image for companionship with you. We thank you for giving us hearts to love and creative gifts to bless one another. How marvelous and glorious you are, far above our knowing, yet living within us, constantly challenging us to reach toward our potential as your highest creation. But you know and understand the struggles that often hold us back. Some here today feel burdened down by pressures of work or school or financial difficulties. Some feel the sting of injustice, of being treated unfairly on the job or in relationships. Others suffer the pain of guilt or rejection or failure. Give us faith to believe that you can turn struggles into triumphs, pain into joy. We pray for those in our community who suffer from physical illness and for those whose hearts ache with grief. Give them comfort and healing according to their deepest needs.

Challenge us all to be more sensitive to the suffering of others: to see you in the poor, the hungry, the frightened, and the lonely. We confess that we are often motivated more by our own desires for prestige, money, and security than by the needs of our sisters and brothers around us. We say we want to show your love, but we act as though only our selfish concerns mattered. Thank you for loving us just as we are, but constantly stirring us to become so much more. Give us determination to develop and use the talents you have given us to bring your peace and healing to our wounded world. Amen.

Amazing, Loving Spirit, we rejoice that you live in each one of us. We cannot logically explain this amazing truth, but we accept it by faith. We know you have been with us, sometimes in dramatic ways and sometimes in quiet, peaceful assurance. And we know that you empower and comfort us. Help us to open our minds and hearts more fully to your life-changing work within us. You know the needs of each one of us. Some here today feel burdened by responsibilities; others feel pressured by financial difficulties. There are those who feel weighed down by physical limitations or illness, and those whose hearts ache with grief or loneliness. Many are searching for meaning and hope. May we all feel your healing love in the depths of our spirits. Help us to use even our painful circumstances to increase our compassion for others who are hurting.

We confess that we often get so caught up in ourselves that we ignore those around us. Sometimes we refuse to look beyond our own worlds because we're afraid of what we will see. We don't want to see hungry children, domestic violence, prejudice, and war. Overwhelmed by all these needs, we sometimes want to despair. Help us to believe that your love is stronger than hate, that peace is stronger than violence. Teach us to be more effective instruments of your world-changing love and peace. Empower and inspire us with faith and hope. Let it be.

Source of all life and blessings, we praise you for your goodness to us. We rejoice in daily reminders of your grace at work. May our gratitude overflow in our gifts to others. Help us to develop our talents to the fullest and to give of our best. Thank you for the encouragement and wisdom we find in this community of faith. We are indeed grateful for all those through the years who have given their talents, time, financial resources, vision, and dedication to this community.

Gracious Friend, we come today lifting our needs to you. You know us far better than we know ourselves. We come in faith, trusting you to supply our deepest needs. We hurt with those who suffer from grief, failure, injustice, loneliness, and physical illness. Give them the comfort and assurance of your loving presence. We all come to you today with our brokenness—broken relationships, broken promises, broken dreams. Touch us with your healing, and reassure us that you are with us and for us through all of life.

Sister-Brother Spirit, who makes all things new, we confess that we often become too comfortable and set in our ways to risk change and growth. Forgive us when we have been self-satisfied and indifferent. Help us to draw renewed faith and hope from our past, but not to rest on past accomplishments. Give us the vision and courage to step out in new directions, the humility to accept and learn from those who differ from us, and the faith to follow wherever you lead us into our needy community. Inspire us to stretch forward to what lies ahead, pressing on in your mission of healing, peace, and justice for all. Amen.

OFFERTORY PRAYERS

Giver of all good gifts, how grateful we are for the wonderful gift of your love. May we express our gratitude not only with our words but also through our actions. Help us to know the joy of generous, faithful giving to you and your ministry through this community. Receive the gifts we bring this day for the spreading of love and hope. Amen.

"To whom much has been given, much will be required" (Luke 12:48). Gracious Giver, you have given so much to us, and we come to give back. But we give not because giving is required, but because giving is delightful. Bless these gifts we bring today. Challenge us to give more generously of our money, talents, and time. So be it!

Sister-Brother Spirit, help us to see your image in all our sisters and brothers. May we see you in those who are poor, hungry, sick, and hurting. Stir our hearts so that we will give generously from the gifts you have given us. Bless these gifts we bring today so that they may be instruments of your peace and love. Amen.

Divine Wisdom, guide our community to use these gifts wisely. We thank you for gifts to give. May we feel the deep joy that comes from giving to your work of peace, justice, and healing in our world. Amen.

You have poured out your Spirit and your gifts upon us. We want to express our gratitude. So we come bringing these offerings for the spread of wisdom and peace in our community and in our world. So be it.

Loving Maker of all, how grateful we are that you stand by us and work for us through all the circumstances of our lives. We have received abundant gifts from you. Help us to give freely and joyfully to others in need. Bless and multiply these offerings for the spread of love and justice and peace. So be it.

$\sim \sim \sim$

May we be motivated by love and gratitude to bring our best gifts to you, Holy Wisdom. For you have given us gifts far more precious than all the silver and gold in the world. Teach us to use your gifts of peace and love to change our community and our world. Bless these offerings we now contribute to your work. Amen.

$\sim \sim \sim$

May the vision and generosity of our mothers and fathers in the faith inspire us to give generously of our gifts. We dare to believe, Mother-Father Creator, that you will multiply these offerings to transform us and our world. So be it!

∽ ∽ ∽

Most generous Giver, as we bring our offerings today, may our hearts be filled with gratitude for your abundant gifts to us. Help us to give not only our money but also our talents and time to your work of love and peace. Teach us to be gracious, generous givers in your image. Let it be!

∽ ∽ ∽

We come to you, Sister-Brother Spirit, with varied gifts of our money, talents, and time. Whatever our gifts, we know that we are responsible to use them for the spread of your love and peace in our community and around the world. Challenge us to give generously. Amen.

∽ ∽ ∽

May these gifts bring hope to those who live in despair, peace to those who live with violence, and justice to those who live in oppression. Grant to each giver a sense of participation in the most important opportunity of all time, sharing Divine Love with the world. To this end, we dedicate our offerings and ourselves. Amen.

∽ ∽ ∽

Infinite Love, these gifts we bring today seem small to us. And yet we know that you accept them and multiply them to bring healing in our world. May our hearts come alive with gratitude for your abundant gifts to us. As we offer our gifts to you today, inspire us to respond with greater generosity. So be it!

Giver of all life and blessings, we want to express our gratitude to you. We struggle at times to know how to do this. We are grateful that you give us tangible ways, like this offering, to say "thank you." These gifts we bring are gifts from you, and we are grateful for this opportunity to give back. Accept our offering as the giving of ourselves for the increase of love and peace in our world. Amen.

You have made us glad by your work; at the works of your hands we sing for joy.[18] We thank you, Maker of all. May our gratitude for your marvelous gifts overflow in our giving this day and always. So be it!

Our Father and Mother, Friend and Guide, you have brought us peace when we are anxious. You have given us hope when we are discouraged. You have put joy in our hearts when we are sad. For these and all your amazing gifts to us, we are indeed grateful. Accept our offerings today as expressions of our gratitude. Amen.

Infinite Wisdom, how magnificent are your gifts to us! We praise you and thank you! As one expression of our gratitude, we bring these offerings today. Bless them and use them for your work in our world. Guide us to join your work of peace. So be it!

Holy One, from whom all blessings flow, we come today with deep gratitude for the diversity of gifts you have given us. We rejoice in the variety of talents and resources in this faith community. Help us to be good stewards of these amazing blessings. May the gifts we bring today bless others. So be it!

We come believing that you can use anything and everything we offer to spread your love in our community and in our world. Thank you, Loving Mother and Father, for this opportunity to give. So many of your children suffer from hunger, poverty, and injustice. Inspire us to give more of our resources and ourselves to your work of restoration. Amen.

Divine Wisdom, you are constantly creating and re-creating, healing and restoring. We want to join your amazing work in our community and in our world. Guide our words and actions. Inspire us to dream your big dreams of peace and justice and liberation for all. Bless these gifts we offer today to help make these dreams reality. So be it!

We come with visions of a new creation, one of peace and wholeness and harmony—of shalom for everyone. Loving Spirit, we rejoice that you live within and among us, giving us power to participate in this new creation. Bless the gifts of talents, time, and money we bring today for this magnificent work! So be it!

BENEDICTIONS/CLOSING BLESSINGS

May we open our minds to unending conversation;
May we open our vision to imagination;
May we open our lives to transformation;
May we join in the Spirit's new creation,
Now and always. So be it!

Go forth with joy and assurance that our Maker will complete the good work begun in us. Let us hold fast our visions, drawing from them power to co-create with Wisdom a world of peace and beauty and justice. May the blessing of the Spirit who empowers life be with us now and forever. Go forth in peace!

Go forth with fresh zeal and confidence and courage to use the Spirit's gifts to the fullest. Go with joy and hope that keeps our dreams alive. Go forth in power and peace!

May the Holy One from whom all blessings flow be with us. May we go forth filled with gratitude that overflows to bless others. May we abide in hope, peace, and joy, now and forever. Amen.

May Divine Wisdom guide us as we go forth on her paths of peace. May she give us blessings more precious than silver or gold.[19] May we find joy in sharing these blessings with others. May Wisdom empower us to change our world! Amen.

May we go out into our broken world to bring healing, peace, and love. May the blessing of the Holy One who gives us life, the blessing of Holy Wisdom who guides our lives, and the blessing of the Holy Spirit who empowers our lives, be with us now and forever. Amen.

Join Divine Wisdom on her paths of peace and justice. Go out into a needy world to spread the good news of love and hope. May Wisdom guide us and empower us now and always. So be it!

May we go out with renewed hope that we can join the Spirit's miraculous work of love in our community and in our world. May we feel the Spirit of Power within us and among us. May we abound in joy and peace, now and forever!

"You shall go out in joy, and be led back in peace; the mountains and the hills before you shall burst into song, and all the trees of the field shall clap their hands" (Isaiah 55:12). Go out in joy and peace!

"Blessed are those who hunger and thirst for righteousness, for they will be filled" (Matthew 5:6). We came hungering and thirsting, and we go away filled. Thank you, Renewing Spirit, for your gifts to us! As we go, inspire us to share your goodness with others. Amen.

May the Spirit of Hope fill us with great joy and peace. Let us take this joy and peace to our broken world. Let us dare to believe that we can join the Spirit's work of transforming our world. Let it be!

Go now in the confidence of the rich treasures of the Creative Spirit within and among us. Celebrate the fullness of our creative power. Go to share our treasures and to give birth to new life. Let it be!

Go now as instruments of peace and grace and justice. Let us send our gifts forth on wings of healing. Go in faith that the Spirit is with us and within us now and forever.

Go with hope and peace filling your hearts. Go with renewed joy in your faith. Go with the power of the Spirit of Life and Love! So be it!

"The fruit of the Spirit is love, joy, peace, patience, kindness, generosity, faithfulness, gentleness, and self-control" (Galatians 5:22–23). May our worship today inspire us to demonstrate the fruit of the Spirit in our lives. Go now with the Spirit! So be it!

"As a mother comforts her child, so I will comfort you" (Isaiah 66:13). Go now in the comfort and peace of the One who gave birth to us. Go in the assurance that the Comforter is with us always. Go to give comfort and peace to others. Amen.

Go forth strengthened with renewed faith in Divine Love that casts out all fears and heals all wounds. Take this Love to a hurting world. Go with the blessed assurance that nothing can ever separate us from this Love. Amen.

Go from this sanctuary out into the temple of creation. Let us go forth praising our Maker for the wonders of creation. May we be open to new revelations at any time and in any place! So be it!

Through this time of worship, we have entered the spiritual dimension of our lives. The Spirit of Life has given us renewed strength and hope. We have received glimpses of a deeper reality. Let us take these glimpses of eternity back into our daily work and play. Amen.

Sister-Brother Spirit, we leave this place today with deep gratitude. For experiences of your healing power, we are grateful. For relationships that nourish and strengthen us, we are grateful. For the beauty of your creation, we are grateful. Show us specific ways in the coming week that we can bless others. Amen.

ENDNOTES

1. Genesis 1:1–24.
2. Genesis 1:31.
3. Isaiah 66:13.
4. Psalm 103:13.
5. Jann Aldredge-Clanton, *Inclusive Hymns for Liberating Christians* (Austin: Eakin Press, 2006), 23.
6. Ibid., 138.
7. Psalm 84:1–4.
8. Isaiah 41:17–18.
9. Psalm 96:1–3.
10. Psalm 118:24.
11. Psalm 92:1–2, 4–5.
12. Matthew 23:37.
13. Micah 6:8.
14. Psalm 95:1–6.
15. Deuteronomy 32:11–12, paraphrase of KJV.
16. Aldredge-Clanton, *Inclusive Hymns*, 91.
17. Proverbs 1, 3.
18. Psalm 92:4.
19. Proverbs 3:13–15, 17.

Inclusive Blessings and Prayers for Varied Settings

EARTH DAY
INTERGENERATIONAL CELEBRATION

Leader: Birth-Giver, we come to thank you for the glorious, abundant life you have brought to our earth. We praise you for the marvelous beauty and variety of life on earth. Divine Wisdom, teach us specific ways we can care for the earth. May our celebration this day also be a commitment to take care of earth's resources.

Adults: Come, let us celebrate the wonders of the earth! Let us rejoice in the glory of each night and day. Let us praise the Giver of Life. Let us give thanks for the abundance of earth.

Children: Come sing and dance and play with joy;
    Earth delights each girl and boy.

All: We celebrate the lovely earth;
    Our Maker brings all life to birth.

Adults: We marvel at the amazing variety of plants and animals, the vastness of earth's resources to sustain us all, the new life that is born daily, our connection with all living beings.

Children: The earth gives us good things to eat,
    And fresh, cool water in the heat.

All: We celebrate the lovely earth;
    Our Maker brings all life to birth.

Adults: Earth lavishes us with sensuous pleasures: iridescent flowers of sweetest scent, luscious fruits flowing with juice, gentle breezes whispering through stately trees.

Children: The earth is filled with fun and glee,
    amazing sights for all to see.

All: We celebrate the lovely earth;
Our Maker brings all life to birth.

Leader: Holy Wisdom, guide us to care for the earth. You have taught us that the resources of the earth are vast, but limited. Show us ways to conserve these resources. Help us discover our connection with all life and to respect the value of other living beings. We know that the earth is wounded and sick. Earth has become polluted with unhealthy waste products. Earth's water, air, and land may not be safe for our children and grandchildren. We are passing down a dangerous environment. Help us to join together with you to bring healing to the earth.

All: We will join Holy Wisdom in her work of restoring the earth. We commit ourselves to work in partnership with Wisdom for a healthy, beautiful earth.

GROUNDBREAKING
OF A NEW WORSHIP PLACE

Source of all blessings, we come here together to celebrate this day we have looked forward to for many years. Today we celebrate the realization of a vision held in the hearts of many people. We celebrate this day of beginning, as we break ground for [name of new place]. We rejoice in this dream come true. For those who have made this great day possible, we are indeed thankful. We are grateful for [name specific people], who had the vision of this new place of worship and who have given of their wisdom, creativity, and time to plan it. For those whose generous gifts have made this place possible, we are grateful. [You may want to name individual or group donors and other specific people instrumental in making the new worship place possible.]

As we come to break this ground, we pray your deepest blessings upon this place. May it truly be holy ground, a sacred place of peace, inspiration, hope, and healing for all who come here. Divine Wisdom, guide those involved in the planning, designing, and constructing of this holy place, and bless all those who contribute in any way. May everyone who comes to this place feel your life-giving presence and peace. We dedicate this sacred place to your amazing love and grace, leading us to become all you created us to be in your divine image. Amen.

THANKSGIVING CELEBRATION

Leader: Sing joyful songs to Ruah,[1] who created the earth and every living being. Praise Ruah! Her presence surrounds us and fills us with goodness and grace. Her love endures forever. Let us celebrate with thanksgiving the marvelous works of Ruah, the Creative Spirit!

All: How great are your works, Creative Spirit; the works of your hands make our hearts glad. It is good to give thanks to you, Giver of all good gifts, to sing praises to your name, to declare your steadfast love in the morning and your faithfulness by night. We rejoice in the beauty of your creation. We sing for joy when we gaze upon earth's splendor.[2]

Leader: Bless Ruah, Spirit of all creation. Ruah, we give thanks to you. Clothed with purple garments of light, you move over land and water, bringing forth multiform life and beauty. Riding on the wings of the wind, you make chariot clouds in the sky. You make the moon to mark the seasons, and the sun to rise at daybreak. You make springs gush forth in the valleys, flowing through the hills, giving drink to every wild animal. Great Creative Spirit, you give grass for the cattle and plants for people to eat. You make mountains for the wild goats and trees for the birds to build their nests. You make the lions roar and the whales sport in the wide seas. You make the darkness of night for the animals of the forest to come out. The earth is filled with your creations, innumerable living beings, both small and large. May your glory endure forever; may you rejoice in all your works. We will praise you as long as we live.[3]

All: Ruah, Spirit of all creation, we come with thanksgiving for your freely flowing gifts that nourish and sustain and enrich our lives. For the continual renewal of our lives through your abundant gifts to us, we are indeed grateful. For gifts to give we are grateful, knowing that as we give we also receive. Dancing in your circle of giving and receiving, we become united with you and with all creation. Sister-Brother Spirit, may we freely give from all that we have received, following your example of creative compassion, justice-making, and peacemaking. We celebrate your presence in fresh ways as we come together in creative partnership. May our gratitude empower us to give generously to meet the needs of people in our community and in our world. So be it!

HOUSE BLESSING

A LITANY OF BLESSING

Leader: We come together to bless this house, the home of [give names of family members]. May this home be a place of peace, security, and love. May it be a place of joy, creative work, refreshing relaxation, and strengthening ties with friends. "How very good and pleasant it is when [people] live together in unity" (Psalm 133:1).

All: May the Creative Spirit fill this home with "love, joy, peace, patience, kindness, generosity, faithfulness, gentleness, and self-control" (Galatians 5:22–23).

Leader: We dedicate this home to love and understanding. May the individuality of each person who lives and visits here be appreciated. May joys and sorrows be shared.

Family members: May we live in this home happily and peacefully and with respect for everyone who comes here.

All: We light a candle to love. (One person lights a candle.) We dedicate this home to loving acceptance of everyone.

Family members: May our home be filled with kindness, tenderness, and understanding.

All: We light a candle to joy. (One person lights a candle.) We dedicate this home to abundant life.

Family members: May our home be filled with joy and laughter.

All: We light a candle to friendship. (One person lights a candle.) We dedicate this home to good times with friends.

Family members: May the doors of our home be open in hospitality.

All: We light a candle to cooperation. (One person lights a candle.) We dedicate the time and talent of those who live here to help build a world in which everyone may have a home of comfort and safety.

Family members: May our home restore our energy to work for the good of others.

All: We light a candle to appreciation. (One person lights a candle.) We dedicate this home to the appreciation of all things good and true and beautiful.

Family members: May the books in our home bring wisdom, the pictures and plants bring beauty, and the music bring inspiration.

All: We light these candles to all other spiritual gifts. (One person lights two candles.) As the flames point upward, so our thoughts rise in gratitude to our Creator for this home and in prayer for divine blessings upon it.

BLESSING WITH HOLY WATER

Leader: In the Jewish and Christian traditions and in other traditions, water has long been a symbol of blessing, of renewal, of healing, and of new life. We will now use this water to bless the home of [give names of family members].

(The group goes from room to room. As the leader blesses each room with the holy water, she or he will speak the words below. Then everyone will repeat these words. Anyone who wishes may also give personal words of blessing.)

Leader, then **All:** May the blessings of Mother-Father Creator and Hokmah-Sophia Wisdom, and Sister-Brother Spirit fill this room with love, joy, and peace, now and always.

Closing Prayer

>**All:** Great Creative Spirit, may we feel you with and within us today as we celebrate this home and those who live here. We rejoice in your abundant life and love that we feel in this home. We pray your deepest blessings upon [give names of family members] and their home, now and always.

BEGINNING A NEW MINISTRY

Reader 1: "For surely I know the plans I have for you, . . . to give you a future with hope" (Jeremiah 29:11).

Reader 2: The Creative Spirit has big plans for us.

All: We can join in these big plans.

Reader 1: Little plans have no magic to stir hope in our hearts.

All: When we make big plans, anything can happen.

Reader 2: So what are these big plans?

All: These big plans connect our gifts and passion with the world's needs. With imagination, courage, and faith, we can translate our plans into actions that bring us hope and joy as we meet people's needs.

Reader 1: Our new ministry of [specific name of ministry] will engage all the gifts and passion we can bring.

Reader 2: This ministry extends our various gifts to meet the needs of many people around us.

All: Sister-Brother Spirit, within and among us, give us power and passion for this new ministry of [name of ministry] we are beginning. May we use our gifts to the fullest to help the people who need us most. Guide us with your wisdom and compassion. We join your big plans for this new ministry!

PRAYER FOR PEOPLE SUFFERING
FROM A HUMAN-MADE DISASTER

(such as September 11 and other acts of terror and violence)

Source of all life, we come together today in this time of great need, calling upon your help. For you are our "refuge and strength, a very present help in trouble" (Psalm 46:1). We join together to bring our prayers to you in this time of deep tragedy. We come as a community to pray for your love and peace to overcome hate and violence in our world. We come deeply grieved that there are those who have attempted to distort your will and have performed acts of devastating destruction. We are distressed over the hatred, bigotry, and injustice that lead to acts of violence. We pray for safety, for cessation of all violence, for peace in our world. As a mother comforts her children, bring your comfort and protection. Holy Wisdom, guide us to overcome injustice and prejudice, and lead us on your pathways of peace. Help the leaders of our world to work together to end violence and bring peace, freedom, and justice to all people. Remembering the words of Dr. Martin Luther King Jr. that "injustice anywhere is a threat to justice everywhere,"[4] we ask that you give us grace to work for justice in our community and in our world so that there may be peace. May we join hands as sisters and brothers in this community and around the world to work for peace and justice, to heal divisions, to break down walls of prejudice, to end oppressive systems. Renew hope within us that good will overcome evil. May we reach out across cultural, ethnic, and religious differences to affirm one another, our common mission and purpose, and our common partnership with you in serving all humanity through your love. Amen.

PRAYER FOR PEOPLE SUFFERING FROM A NATURAL DISASTER

(such as hurricanes, earthquakes, tornadoes, and tsunamis)

Hear words of hope and comfort from the prophet Isaiah:

> Thus says the [One] who created you, [the One] who formed you. . . . "Do not fear, for I have redeemed you; I have called you by name, you are mine. When you pass through the waters, I will be with you; and through the rivers, they shall not overwhelm you; when you walk through fire, you shall not be burned, and the flame shall not consume you.
>
> As a mother comforts her child, so I will comfort you; you shall be comforted" (Isaiah 43:1–2; 66:13).

O Loving Spirit, we come calling out to you for help for those suffering from the destruction of [name hurricane, earthquake, tornado, or other natural disaster]. We come believing that you hear the cries of those who need to be rescued from danger, those in desperate need of physical aid and medical care. We believe you also understand their need for emotional and spiritual help to live through this tragedy. Bring your help and comfort to all those who are suffering. There are so many things we don't understand in this life, but we come in faith that you created us all, that you call each of us by name, that we are all precious to you, and that your love is deeper than we can imagine.

We know that your loving care especially reaches to the poor, the orphaned, the widowed, and those in distress, and that any help we give our sisters and brothers in need, we are also giving to you. We believe you hear the cries of all those in distress in [name place/s] and other areas hit by [name of disaster]. Come to their aid. Send rescue and medical workers quickly to help, and give them guidance and strength for their life-saving work. You have called us to help, to "weep with those who weep" (Romans 12:15). So we come joining with you to reach out to those who are suffering. Divine Wisdom, lead us to specific ways we can help those in distress. Give us your strength and comfort as we reach out in your holy name. Amen.

HEALING MEDITATION

Close your eyes and begin taking slow, deep breaths. Inhale slowly, counting to eight. Exhale slowly, counting to ten. Breathe in deeply and slowly through your nose . . . and breathe out slowly through your mouth. Continue inhaling through your nose to the count of eight and exhaling through your mouth to the count of ten. Breathe in deeply, filling your whole body-soul with the Spirit of Peace. Breathe out slowly, letting go of all that blocks peace in your life . . . breathing in . . . and breathing out . . . slowly . . . and deeply, feeling the Spirit of Peace within you and surrounding you.

Breathe in slowly and deeply, filling your whole body-soul with the Spirit of Wisdom. Breathe out slowly, letting go of all that blocks wisdom in your life. Breathe deeply and slowly, in and out.

As you keep breathing slowly and deeply, in and out, visualize a healing light entering your head and moving throughout your body. Breathing in . . . and breathing out . . . feel the healing light flowing through your body . . . from your head to your feet. Breathe in healing power. Breathe out all that limits the healing power within you.

Breathe in peace. Breathe out tension and stress. Breathe in love. Breathe out fear. Breathe in healing. Breathe out disease. Feel deep love and healing flowing through every cell of your body, bringing peace and healing. Feel healing peace . . . healing love . . . healing power flowing freely through your body-soul. Breathe in the Spirit that flows through all creation, now freely flowing through you as you breathe in . . . and breathe out. Feel the healing power within you, now flowing out to others. Visualize those whom you want to surround with this healing power.

Loving Healer, we claim your healing power within and among us. Divine Wisdom, lead us on your paths to healing and wholeness. Give your healing grace to all those we have visualized and others on our hearts today. Bring us all healing according to our deepest needs of body, mind, and spirit. We come with gratitude that you have called us to be partners in your healing work. Open our eyes to our individual and collective power as ministers of healing and grace. Challenge us to continue stretching toward all you created us to be in your own image. Amen.

TRANSITION OF A COLLEAGUE
TO A NEW MINISTRY

OPENING PRAYER

Leader 1: Gracious Giver of all gifts, we come today with gratitude for your gift of our colleague, [person's name]. We are indeed grateful for [her/his] dedicated ministry to a diversity of people here at [name community or organization the person is leaving]. We celebrate [his/her] gifts of leadership, compassion, wisdom, and diligence [change or add other gifts of this person]. Thank you for the gifts of your Spirit within [person's name], bringing blessing and grace to all around [her/him]. We come also with sadness because we will miss [him/her] on the team here at [name community or organization the person is leaving]. But we join [him/her] in expectation of many new, exciting adventures. Bless [person's name] with success in future endeavors, as [she/he] continues to claim [her/his] gifts and calling. And bless us all as we continue to become all you created us to be in your own image, now and always.

RESPONSIVE BLESSING (FROM PROVERBS 2–4)

Leader 1: Happy are those who find wisdom, and those who get understanding, for her income is better than silver, and her revenue better than gold.

All: She is more precious than jewels, and nothing you desire can compare with her. Long life is in her right hand; in her left hand are riches and honor.

Leader 2: Her ways are ways of pleasantness, and all her paths are peace.

All: She is a tree of life to those who lay hold of her; those who hold her fast are called happy.

Leader 1: Wisdom will come into your heart, and will be pleasant to your soul.

All: Do not forsake her, and she will keep you; love her, and she will guard you.

Leader 2: Prize her highly, and she will exalt you; she will honor you if you embrace her.

All: She will place on your head a fair garland; she will bestow on you a beautiful crown.

Leader 1: Today we come to celebrate the work of Divine Wisdom in the life of [person's name]. We come in gratitude for [her/his] abundant gifts and graces and all the ways [she/he] has used them in [her/his] ministry of [name specific ministry the person is leaving]. [Person's name] is a minister of Wisdom in numerous ways. [She/He] is a healer, a counselor, a preacher, a teacher, a leader, a prophet, a peacemaker, a friend [change or add other ministry descriptions for this person]. [Person's name] has also blessed all of us and so many others with [her/his] gifts of creativity, compassion, sense of humor, leadership, and enthusiasm [change or add other gifts of this person]. And we celebrate [his/her] continual openness to new ideas and adventures in ministry. We come now to bless [person's name] as [he/she] begins a new chapter in [his/her] ministry.

All: [Person's name], we celebrate your call and your abundant gifts. We thank our Mother-Father Creator for all the ways you have blessed a diversity of people in your ministry here. We're grateful for your outstanding contributions to [name the community or organization the person is leaving]. We pray Wisdom's deepest blessings on you as you begin your new ministry of [name the ministry the person is beginning].

Leader 2: [Person's name], we celebrate the gifts of Wisdom in you, bringing blessing and grace to all around you.

All: May our Loving Maker bless you as you continue to fulfill your call. May Sister-Brother Spirit continue to give you power, wisdom, and hope to make your visions reality.

PERSONAL WORDS OF BLESSING

(Participants, who so desire, speak personal words of blessing to the person in transition to a new ministry.)

CLOSING PRAYER

Leader 2: Loving Maker, our strong and tender Mother and Father, we come today to celebrate the ministry of [person's name] and to ask your blessings on [her/him] as [she/he] begins new adventures. Thank you for [person's name] and all [his/her] gifts that will continue to bless everyone [he/she] has touched through [his/her] ministry here. May [person's name] feel the reward of knowing that [she/he] has made a difference in the lives of so many people to whom [she/he] has been your minister of hope and healing. We're also indeed grateful for all the ways [person's name] has blessed us, [her/his] colleagues. Now we ask your deepest blessings on [person's name] as [he/she] moves to a new ministry. Divine Wisdom, Sophia, guide [person's name] as [he/she] continues to fulfill [his/her] ministry call. May your Spirit within [person's name] continue to give [her/him] power, wisdom, and hope to make [her/his] visions reality. Amen.

WISDOM'S BLESSINGS

(from Ecclesiasticus 1; Wisdom 7 and 8)

Leader: The sand of the seas and the raindrops, and the days of eternity, who can assess them? The breadth of the earth and the depth of the universe, who can probe them?

All: Wisdom created the universe and all that is within. Wisdom brings all good things to us. She is an inexhaustible treasure.

Leader: Wisdom teaches us the structure of the world and the properties of the elements, the alternation of the solstices and the succession of the seasons, the revolution of the year and the positions of the stars, the natures of animals and the instincts of wild beasts, the powers of spirits and the mental processes of human beings, the varieties of plants and the medical properties of roots. All that is hidden, all that is plain, we learn from Wisdom, who designed them all.

All: Within Wisdom is a spirit intelligent, holy, unique, manifold, subtle, active, incisive, unsullied, lucid, invulnerable, benevolent, sharp, beneficent, loving, steadfast, dependable, unperturbed, almighty, pure. For Wisdom is quicker to move than any motion. She pervades and permeates all things. She can do all. Herself unchanging, she makes all things new.

Leader: In each generation Wisdom passes into holy souls; she makes them friends of the Eternal and the prophets. She is indeed more splendid than the sun; she outshines all the constellations. Over Wisdom nothing can ever triumph.

All: Wisdom sends her strength from one end of the earth to the other, ordering all things for good. O Wisdom, come to us! Pour out your blessings on us!

LAMENTING INJUSTICES

All: Life-Giver, we cry out to you in our pain and distress. We wonder if you hear our cries and see our anguish. We have been harassed and abused. We suffer from prejudice and misunderstanding. Our bodies suffer pain, and our hearts suffer grief. All around, people are suffering from poverty, hunger, and violence. We wonder if you care. "Rouse yourself! Why do you sleep? Awake, do not cast us off forever! Why do you hide your face? Why do you forget our affliction and oppression? For we sink down to the dust; our bodies cling to the ground. Rise up, come to our help. Redeem us for the sake of your steadfast love" (Psalm 44:23–26).

Group 1: Without justice, there can be no healing and no peace. There is no justice when women, men, and children suffer from poverty and abuse.

Group 2: There is no justice when people suffer from hunger and violence.

Group 1: There is no justice when people suffer from discrimination because of gender, race, class, sexual orientation, disability, religion.

All: We have all suffered from injustice and abuse. Growing up in patriarchal religions and cultures, we have been devalued, demeaned, stifled, and ignored.

Women: Women have suffered abuse and discrimination. We have been physically, emotionally, and spiritually raped. Our sacred power has been denied by religious institutions that exclude women from leadership and exclude the Divine Feminine from worship. Our minds have been devalued, and our bodies have been objectified.

Men: Men, especially men of color and homosexual men, have suffered abuse and discrimination. Patriarchal religion and culture, though exalting maleness, have also taken their toll on us. Our emotions have been stifled, and our physical strength has been exalted.

Group 2: We live in a society that rapes the earth, scorns the feminine, and worships the masculine. By denying Deity a female face, our culture denies the value of the feminine in ourselves and in all creation.

All: We all suffer from injustice and abuse. Our bodies, minds, and spirits feel the wounds of long abuse. There can be no justice until all forms of sexism, racism, classism, heterosexism, and ableism are eliminated. We cry out for justice and healing.

Group 1: Justice and healing will come as we open ourselves to new revelations that revalue all women, men, and children—all creation.

Group 2: Sacred symbols give deepest value. Justice and healing will come as we give equal value to women and men, to girls and boys by giving equal value to female and male sacred symbols. We have a long way to go, but we are on the journey toward recovery.

All: Sister-Brother Spirit, we cry out for healing now! Help us to claim your power within us so that together we may rise to wholeness of life. Bring justice and peace to our world so that all beings can become the joy-filled creation you intended, now and always.

LAMENTING VIOLENCE AGAINST WOMEN AND GIRLS

(As each voice reads, a chorus of women chant softly in the background: "Stop, stop, stop the violence against women.")

Voice 1: During the Inquisition, an estimated two hundred thousand to nine million women were burned as "witches."[5] We cry out against this shocking nightmare, these horrible crimes against women. This holocaust of women has not been remembered. Now we remember and mourn this holocaust of women.

All (loudly): Stop, stop, stop the violence against women and girls.

Voice 2: Throughout history women and girls have been killed, beaten, raped, and deprived of human rights.

All (loudly): Stop, stop, stop the violence against women and girls.

Voice 3: In the United States alone, every 15 seconds a woman is battered.[6]

All (loudly): Stop, stop, stop the violence against women.

Voice 4: Every day in the U.S., more than three women are murdered by their husbands or boyfriends.[7]

All (loudly): Stop, stop, stop the violence against women.

Voice 5: In the U.S. alone, women experience an estimated 4.8 million partner-related physical assaults and rapes every year.[8]

All (loudly): Stop, stop, stop the violence against women.

Voice 6: One in six American women has been the victim of attempted or completed rape in her lifetime.[9]

All (loudly): Stop, stop, stop the violence against women.

Voice 7: In the U.S., more than half of all rapes of women occur before age 18; 22 percent occur before age 12.[10]

All (loudly): Stop, stop, stop the violence against women and girls.

Voice 1: One in three women around the world has been beaten, coerced into sex, or otherwise abused in her lifetime.[11]

All (loudly): Stop, stop, stop the violence against women.

Voice 2: For girls and women around the world aged 15 to 44 years, violence is a major cause of death and disability.[12]

All (loudly): Stop, stop, stop the violence against women and girls.

Voice 3: An estimated three million women and girls each year are victims of female genital mutilation, predominately in parts of Africa.[13]

All (loudly): Stop, stop, stop the violence against women and girls.

Voice 4: Worldwide, five thousand women and girls are murdered each year in so-called honor killings by members of their own families.[14]

All (loudly): Stop, stop, stop the violence against women and girls.

Voice 5: Worldwide, an estimated four million women and girls each year are bought and sold into prostitution, slavery, or marriage.[15]

All (loudly): Stop, stop, stop the violence against women and girls.

Voice 6: At least 60 million girls are "missing" from various populations, especially in Asia, as a result of sex-selective abortions, infanticide, or neglect.[16]

All (loudly): Stop, stop, stop the violence against girls.

Voice 7: Seventy percent of the world's poor are women, two out of three children not in school are girls, and women own only one percent of the world's titled land.[17]

All (louder): Stop, stop, stop the violence against women and girls!
NO. NO. NO!
Say NO to violence against women and girls!

Chorus of Women: "Wisdom cries out in the street; in the squares she raises her voice. At the busiest corner she cries out; at the entrance of the city gates she speaks: 'How long, O simple ones, will you love being simple? How long will scoffers delight in their scoffing and fools hate knowledge? Give heed to my reproof; I will pour out my thoughts to you; I will make my words known to you'" (Proverbs 1:20–23), O Feminine Divine Wisdom, you also have been scoffed at, abused, and demeaned. You hear and understand the cries of women around the world. We join you on your "paths of peace." We come to you, our "tree of life" (Proverbs 3:17–18). We join your work of stopping violence against women and girls. With you, we cry out: "No more violence against women and girls!"

CALL TO JUSTICE AND PEACEMAKING

Reader 1: "Is not this the fast that I choose: to loose the bonds of injustice, to undo the thongs of the yoke, to let the oppressed go free, and to break every yoke? Is it not to share your bread with the hungry, and bring the homeless poor into your house; when you see the naked, to cover them, and not to hide yourself from your own kin? Then your light shall break forth like the dawn, and your healing shall spring up quickly" (Isaiah 58:6–8).

Reader 2: "Injustice anywhere is a threat to justice everywhere."[18]

Reader 3: If we do nothing when we see people being treated unfairly because of sexism, racism, heterosexism, classism, ableism, or any other prejudice, we threaten justice for everyone.

All: When we speak out against injustice, we all experience healing. When we break the bonds of injustice, we all experience healing. When we share with the poor and hungry, we help create a better world for everyone.

Reader 1: Without justice, there can be no peace.

Reader 2: When we help break the bonds of injustice and care for the poor, we contribute to peace and healing in our world.

Reader 3: "Blessed are the peacemakers, for they will be called children of God" (Matthew 5:9).

All: We can help create a world of justice and peace, a world of shalom.

Reader 1: "Steadfast love and faithfulness will meet; righteousness and peace will kiss each other" (Psalm 85:10).

Reader 2: "The fruit of the Spirit is love, joy, peace, patience, kindness, generosity, faithfulness, gentleness, and self-control" (Galatians 5:22–23).

Reader 3: "For you shall go out in joy, and be led back in peace; the mountains and the hills before you shall burst into song, and all the trees of the field shall clap their hands" (Isaiah 55:12).

All: We can help create a world of justice and peace, a world of shalom.

Reader 1: Wisdom guides us to bring justice and peace to our world.

Reader 2: "Happy are those who find Wisdom, and those who get understanding, for her income is better than silver, and her revenue better than gold" (Proverbs 3:13–14).

Reader 3: "Her ways are ways of pleasantness, and all her paths are peace" (Proverbs 3:17).

All: Guide us, Holy Wisdom, to follow your paths of peace. Teach us your ways of justice that lead to peace. Give us your vision of a new world of justice and peace. Open our hearts and minds to ways we can help to make this vision a reality. Then the healing of all creation will "spring up quickly." Let it be!

CALL TO FREEDOM

Group 1: Is there liberty anywhere that people suffer from poverty and hunger?

Group 2: Is there justice where people of color earn far less than their white brothers and sisters?

Group 1: Is there liberty where people suffer abuse and discrimination in the marketplace and even in church because of race, gender, sexual orientation, disability, and class?

Group 2: We will speak our visions of a world where we can all be free at last.

Group 1: Our words carry power to overcome prejudice, injustice, violence, and discrimination.

Group 2: Our words carry great power to create and define reality.

Group 1: Our words carry great power to heal our broken world and to create a world of justice and freedom for all.

Group 2: We will speak our visions into reality.

Group 1: We will sing our visions into reality.

Group 2: We will dance our visions into reality.

Group 1: We will act our visions into reality.

Group 2: Let us begin by joining together in speaking our vision, in sounding our call to freedom.

All: We envision a world where the truth that all people are created equal will become a reality. Our vision is of a world where "liberty and justice for all" is more than a pledge. Our vision is of a world where women and men of all races, abilities, and sexual orientations will share equally in opportunities and blessings. We envision an end to war not only across the seas but in our own city streets, an end to abuse of all kinds on the job and in the home. Our vision includes faith communities in which all share equally in leadership and ministry, communities that give sacred value to women and men, to girls and boys by including female as well as male divine images. We envision a world free of discrimination and injustice in any form. We sound a call to freedom in our institutions and in our homes. We call for individual freedom from external definition, freedom to follow the voice within. We call for freedom to love, to create, to laugh, to learn, to grow, to become all we are meant to be.

Leader: Spirit of Freedom and Justice, who has liberated people down through the ages, we call on you today. You are the author of the ideals of "liberty and justice for all," of being "created equal" and endowed with "inalienable rights." But the reality is that people in our country and throughout the world still suffer injustice and discrimination. Help us to work to make justice and equality more than just beautiful words. While we praise the gift of liberty, we also confess that we often prefer security to freedom and responsibility. May we claim the internal freedom and courage to speak out for justice and to work for those changes that would bring true equality of opportunity to all your children. We come today, needing freedom in many areas of our lives. Free us from anxiety, fear, guilt, and everything that keeps us from being the free and powerful people you created us to be. May we all experience more fully your Truth that sets us free, now and always.

DIVERSITY CELEBRATION

(from Psalms 104 and 148)

Leader: How manifold are the works of Hokmah-Sophia Wisdom, marvelous Maker of all!

All: Hokmah-Sophia Wisdom loves variety.

Leader: The earth is full of wonderful creatures, innumerable living beings both small and large.

All: Wisdom, our Maker, loves variety.

Leader: Springs gush forth in fertile valleys, nourishing all kinds of wild animals.

All: Hokmah-Sophia Wisdom loves variety.

Leader: Tall mountains provide homes for wild goats, and the rocks give shelter to the coneys.

All: Wisdom, our Maker, loves variety.

Leader: The earth is filled with cedars and abundant fruit trees, storks and all kinds of flying birds and creeping animals.

All: Hokmah-Sophia Wisdom loves variety.

Leader: Human beings come in a huge variety of races, ages, and sizes. No two people have the same fingerprints.

All: Wisdom, our Maker, loves variety.

Leader: Couples, families, and communities of many shapes and styles fill the world with love and laughter.

All: Hokmah-Sophia Wisdom loves variety.

Leader: But we have not always loved the variety that Wisdom has created.

All: Wisdom, our Maker, forgive our petty striving to squeeze you and your creation into our conventions and traditions.

Forgive us for not recognizing you in all the diversity of your creation. Our ignorance and prejudice have kept us from seeing the sacredness of all you have created. Though you created us with wondrous diversity, we have tried to restrict one another into limited ways of being and doing, and we are all the losers. Forgive us and heal us of our racism, sexism, heterosexism, classicism, ableism, and all other evils that keep us from appreciating your abundant, manifold creation.

Leader: Let us covenant with Hokmah-Sophia Wisdom and with one another to celebrate and nurture diversity.

All: Divine Wisdom, you have created innumerable living beings, beyond our ability to fathom or classify. You have created female and male human beings in a wide variety of rich colors and shapes to show forth your lavishness. You have created people to express sexuality in different ways. Families and communities of diverse forms, religions, and cultures fill the world with joy and grace. Holy Wisdom, we covenant with you and with one another to celebrate and nurture all this diversity.

Leader: Hokmah-Sophia Wisdom fills the world with amazing diversity!

All: Wisdom, our Maker, we covenant with you and with one another to celebrate and nurture all this diversity, now and always!

WISE AGING CELEBRATION

(Play classical music in the background. If the setting is conducive, create an altar with classic works of literature and art and pictures of respected older people, like Dr. Dorothy Height and Dr. Nelson Mandela.)

OPENING PRAYER

Leader: Divine Wisdom, we come to celebrate your growing power in us as we grow older. Guide us to become wiser as we grow older. We feel the urgency of time and want to use our precious moments wisely, but help us to know when to rest as well as when to work. May we accept our limitations without using them as excuses to keep from growing and creating. Holy Wisdom, lead us to new adventures that draw from your deep creative wells within us. Give us new visions and missions that challenge us to expand our gifts. Teach us when to say "No" to those things that drain our energy, so that we can say "Yes" to those ventures that engage our fullest gifts to meet the world's needs. Help us to take good care of our bodies, minds, and spirits. May we grow in compassion, creativity, peace, and love. We celebrate all we are moving toward. Ancient Wisdom, open our eyes to discover new meaning and purpose as we age wisely and well in your image. Empower us to continue to blossom into all you created us to be, now and always.

RESPONSIVE BLESSING

Group 1: Music, art, and literature that have stood the test of time are given respect as "classics." We put the highest value on wine that has aged. But many cultures do not value aging people.

Group 2: Today we come to honor and bless aging people, including all of us, whether we realize we are aging or not.

Group 1: From the time we are born, we are "aging." We consider this "aging" a good thing until we reach a certain age, which some cultures label as "over the hill."

Group 2: Today we come to honor and bless one another, wherever we are in the aging process. We are valuable just as we are, without trying to look or act younger than we are.

Group 1: Biblical revelation places great value on aging. In ancient Israel those who held positions of authority were "elders." These older people performed important tasks in the community. In the early Christian community the leaders were "elders," serving as decision-makers and ministers. Scripture equates aging with Wisdom (*Hokmah* in Hebrew, *Sophia* in Greek), a personification of Deity. Wisdom gives age sacred value because she is older than the earth. Wisdom says, "Ages ago I was set up, at the first, before the beginning of the earth" (Proverbs 8:23). Wisdom is old. Old people have wisdom.

Group 2: Today we bless our aging, embracing the wisdom we have gained through our years. We honor and value ourselves as we change and grow. Our aging leads to deeper and fuller wisdom.

All: We bless one another as we age. We are becoming wise elders and classics. As we age, we are gaining valuable wisdom that our world needs. Embracing the gifts of each moment, we discover new meaning and new creativity. At every age, our lives are filled with possibility. "The righteous flourish like the palm tree, and grow like a cedar in Lebanon. . . . In old age they still produce fruit; they are always green and full of sap" (Psalm 92:12, 14). "I will pour out my Spirit upon all flesh, and your sons and your daughters shall prophesy, and your young [people] shall see visions, and your old [people] shall dream dreams" (Acts 2:17).

CLOSING PRAYER

Leader: Ancient Wisdom, Hokmah-Sophia, open our eyes to new visions and missions as we age. May we dream dreams of bringing your justice and peace on earth. Divine Wisdom, may we see in you the sacred value of age. Guide us to age wisely as we continue to become all you created us to be in your own image. So be it!

BLESSING OUR CREATIVITY

Leader: Loving Birth-Giver, Holy Ruah,[19] you brought us into this world full of joy, wonder, and possibility. Your laughter filled our souls as we ran freely through fields of splendor, feasting our eyes on bluebonnets iridescent in spring sunlight, drinking from sparkling rivers, smelling sweet honeysuckle, singing with the meadowlarks, rolling down hills of fresh-mowed grass.

All: But somewhere along the way we lost our senses. Instead of "Try it," we heard, "Stop! Be careful!" We have been molded and shaped into neat boxes by those too fearful of the free spirit in us and in themselves.

Leader: Holy Ruah, Creative Spirit, some of your children have been stifled and squeezed almost to the point of destroying your life within them. Broken by violence and abuse and neglect, they cry out, and we cry with them.

All: We are all on the path to recovery from abuse of our creative souls. Our spirits, though weakened, live on. Our childlike wonder, though stifled, lies deep within us. Our creative power, though buried, can rise again to new life and freedom. Creative Spirit, bring our creativity back to life. Inspire us with your playful energy. Guide us with your wisdom. Fill us with your overflowing beauty, now and always.

Leader: Ruah, Holy Beauty, you beckon us through the clatter and clutter, whispering through the gentle spring breeze, calling us to stop and notice.

All: Divine Beauty shouts through flaming rose sunsets, singing through purple and yellow fields of glistening wildflowers, and we still do not notice.

Leader: Beauty shines and sings through all creation, for those open to the holiness in every blade of grass and the music in the smallest insect's voice.

All: Holy Beauty sings through all nature. The universe vibrates with the music of the spheres.

Leader: Static may interrupt and threaten to overwhelm, but the music overcomes, and the truth plays on in purest strains.

All: Thoughtless hands may mar and scar, but the splendor shines through, and the freshness blooms again.

Leader: Holy Beauty, you keep calling us to join you in giving birth, to come alive to the Creative Spirit within us, to bring forth beauty in all we touch.

All: Holy Beauty, you call us to notice and to nurture, to claim the fullness of our creative power, to co-create with you a world beyond imagining.

Leader: Come, Holy Beauty, stir our full humanity that we may know we embody you. All our diversity mirrors your truth and grace; all races show your lovely hue.

All: Come, Holy Beauty, waken our divinity that we may be your image fair, clothed in your dignity, wisdom, and liberty, creative power with you to share.[20]

ENDNOTES

1. The Hebrew word for "Spirit" is the feminine word *Ruah.*
2. Psalm 92:1–5.
3. Psalm 104.
4. Martin Luther King Jr., "Letter from Birmingham Jail" (April 16, 1963), in *Why We Can't Wait* (New York: Penguin Books, 1964), 77.
5. Jeanne Achterberg, *Woman as Healer* (Boston: Shambhala Publications, 1990), 85.
6. "Broken Bodies, Shattered Minds: The Global Epidemic of Violence

against Women," *International Journal of Epidemiology* 30 (2001) 649–52. Online: http://ije.oxfordjournals.org/cgi/reprint/30/3/649.pdf.

7. Bureau of Justice Statistics Crime Data Brief, "Intimate Partner Violence, 1993–2001" (February 2003). Online: http://www.pcusa.org/womensadvocacy /issues/violenceagainstwomen/stats.htm#back7.

8. Centers for Disease Control and Prevention, "Understanding Intimate Partner Violence" (2006). Online: http://www.cdc.gov/ncipc/dvp/ipv_fact-sheet.pdf.

9. Patricia Tjaden and Nancy Thoenness, "Prevalence, Incidence, and Consequences of Violence against Women: Findings from the National Violence against Women Survey," National Institute of Justice Centers for Disease Control and Prevention (November 1998), 2. Online: http://www .ncjrs.gov/pdffiles/172837.pdf.

10. Ibid.

11. United Nations General Assembly, "In-Depth Study on All Forms of Violence against Women: Report of the Secretary General, 2006," A/61/122 /Add.1 (July 6, 2006). Online: http://www.unifem.org/gender_issues /violence_against_women/.

12. Parliamentary Assembly of the Council of Europe 2002, "Recommendation 1582 on Domestic Violence against Women" (2002). Online: http://www.unifem.org/gender_issues/violence_against_women /facts_figures.php.

13. United Nations Children's Fund, "Female Genital Mutilation/Cutting: A Statistical Exploration" (New York: UNICEF, 2005), 4.

14. The United Nations Population Fund, The State of World Population 2000 report, "Lives Together, Worlds Apart: Men and Women in a Time of Change" (2000). Online: http://www.unfpa.org/swp/2000/english/ch03.html.

15. Ibid.

16. Ibid.

17. Louise Arbour, United Nations High Commissioner for Human Rights, "International Women's Day: Laws and 'Low Intensity' Discrimination against Women" (March 8, 2008). Online: http://www.ohchr.org/EN/NewsEvents /Pages/DisplayNews.aspx?NewsID=8629&LangID=E.

18. King, "Letter from Birmingham Jail," 77.

19. *Ruah* is the word for "Spirit" in the Hebrew Scriptures (e.g. Genesis 1:2).

20. Jann Aldredge-Clanton, *Inclusive Hymns for Liberating Christians* (Austin: Eakin Press, 2006), 100.